Praise for *The Becket List* Volu

'The book that 2020 desperately nee
the coffee table, the nightstand, the b   , plane, you name
it. Major and minor embuggerances galore in this irreverent
A–Z that combines the genius of Tony Husband's cartoons with
Henry Becket's wry and hilarious observations'

'Witty and fantastically observed… A great gift for the those
who are impossible to buy for or do the same as me and keep it
for yourself!'

'I absolutely loved this book. The author is extremely funny
and it's a really clever, interesting read as well, so much fun with
endless laughs throughout… Highly recommended!'

'Manages to find something amusing in so much of the day-to-
day stuff that almost everyone finds supremely irritating…with
some terrific cartoons too!'

'Perfect for those of us with short attention spans and many
gripes with the world. It is impossible not to feel Becket's
annoyance with those little things that wind us all up'

'Lovely quality hardback, the perfect size to sit on the shelf
beside your loo and amuse'

'So angry, but SO funny. Laugh out loud moments and we
certainly need a lot of these at the moment'

'This is a hilarious, witty guide that will find a good home
in many a downstairs loo library. It's the ultimate gift for the
grumpy git in your life'

'An observation of First World problems for the Victor Meldrew
in your life'

'This is exactly the kind of book that makes the ideal present for the whingers in your life'

'A book that sums up life's little inconveniences and aggravations in perfect form! Fabulously grumpy!'

'In the current climate of Zoom meetings, keeping a copy on your desk to read whilst waiting for the host to let you in is my recommendation'

'I found myself in fits of laughter at some sections, even walking around the house, reading passages out loud to share what was written… It'll definitely lift your mood on a bad day… An ideal secret Santa gift for a colleague or that grumpy relative'

'The perfect coffee table read… A superb book to dip in and out of between books and when you just need a good belly chuckle'

'This is a fabulous book that canters through the many little things that annoy everyone… It is fresh and witty and makes you see the world in a new light – but always with a wry smile'

'It made me laugh out loud. It's well written and kept my attention. Highly recommended'

'I loved this book – [it] brings together all my gripes, moans and frustrations in products and people around me'

'Could not put it down as I found myself agreeing with every single item on his list. Very happy to find somebody quite as grumpy as I am. A real tonic in these bizarre times'

THE BECKET LIST VOLUME II

Even More First World Problems

HENRY BECKET
ILLUSTRATED BY TONY HUSBAND

Dedicated to all those who bought, read or circulated Volume I of The Becket List, *and who have thus, knowingly or unknowingly, continued to provide misplaced encouragement*

Published by Ideas at Work Ltd.

Text © 2022 Henry Becket
Illustrations © 2022 Tony Husband

The right of Henry Becket to be identified as author of this Work has been asserted by him in accordance with sections 77 and 78 of the Copyright, Designs and Patents Act 1988

ISBN 9798378522279

All rights reserved. No part of this publication may be reproduced, stored in a retrieval system, copied in any form or by any means, electronic, mechanical, photocopying, recording or otherwise transmitted without written permission from the author

A CIP catalogue record for this book is available from the British Library

Cover illustration: Tony Husband

Cover and internal design:
sheerdesignandtypesetting.com

Contents

Introduction 15

A

Absence of worthwhile signs amongst a forest of unnecessary ones	17
Absurdly dramatic yawning in public	18
Absurdly over-complicated menu descriptions	19
'Accessible Toilets'	19
Adults with 'sippy cups'/ neo baby bottles	19
Affecting to be something/ someone you're not	20
Age-inappropriate clothing	20
Airfix	21
Airport shops	22
Air travel	22
Alcohol content of wine	23
Ale in cans	23
Alexa	24
Allergies	24
Americanisms	26
Apologising for no reason	26
Apple	26
Arndale Centres	27
'Around…'	27
Assumptive form-filling rubrics	28
Au pairs	28
Auto responses to email	29
Awaydays	29

B

'Back to School'	31
Backwards baseball caps	31
Bad coffee	32
Badly made spritzers	32
Badly packaged bacon… prosciutto…salami…etc	33
Bad manners	33
Bad menu translations	34
Bad spelling etc	35
Bad taste	36
Barista	36
Baseball caps	36
Bathrooms	36
Being told what to do by your car	37
Best practice	37
Birds relieving themselves on your just-cleaned car	38
Birmingham	38
Bloody car drivers who sneak up on your inside before pulling into the sensible gap you'd left behind the car in front	38
Blush wine	39
Books	39
Bottled water	39
Bowties	39
Bum cracks	39

C

Cackling	41
Call centres	41
Cancel culture	42
Candles in jars that stop working when they're a quarter of the way through	44
'Can I get…?'	44
Car names	45
Car rear-ends	45
Chains of coffee shops	45
Children kicking the back of your seat on a flight	46
Children's shoes	46
Chilled ale	46
Chocolates on pillows	47
Christmas tree lights	47
Cider	48
Clinking glasses	48
Clothes on animals	49
C of E	49
Coffee bores and incompetents	49
Coffee shops	50
Cohort	51
Cold blocks in the freezer that are itching to jump out	51
Cold potatoes	51
Collagen	52
Commentators	52
Committees	52
Common cold	53
Complicated door handles	53
Concrete	53
Constant changes to dietary advice	54
Content warnings	54
Corkscrews	55
Crazy paving	55
Creamer	55
Cruise liners	56
Cultural appropriation	57
Culture	57
Cummerbunds	58
Cussedness/contrariness for the sake of it	58
Cut flowers	60
Cycle helmets	61
Cyclists	61

D

Defence procurement	63
Designer handbags	63
Dijon mustard	64
Disappearing hairbrushes	65
Doorhandles	65
Dramatic gum-chewing	65
Dramatic public sneezing	66
Drivers, crap	66
Dummies	66

E

Eating in theatres, cinemas and similarly inappropriate venues	69
Eco-friendly firelighters	69
Eco setting	70
Eggs	70
Egregious	70

Electric lawnmowers	70	Exposed bum cracks	72
Espadrilles	71		

F

Facebook	75	Fellow guests on the lookout for someone more interesting	80
Fake bald heads	76	Film credits	80
Fake bows on Christmas wrapping	77	Fingernails	81
Fake bowties	77	Finishing time of live performances	82
Familiarity	78	Flatpack furniture	82
Far more different kinds of lightbulbs than can really be necessary	78	Flowers	84
		Foodservice manuals	84
Fatuous pronouncements over public address systems	78	French bureaucracy	85
		French lavatories	86
Fatuous questions	79	Full sex	87
Feet on seats	79		

G

Garden centres	89	Grim places of work	91
Gin	89	Gripper rods	92
Grazing	89	Grotesque over-packaging of things purchased online	92
Great sportsmen who are subsequently inappropriately hired as commentators	90	Gum-chewing	92

H

Haggling, twenty-first-century style	95	Having to listen to other people's audible books	97
Hairbrushes	95	Having to show your boarding card at airport shops	98
Hair products	96	Home decorating	98
Half-term trips	96	Houseflies	98
Harem pants	97		
Harrods	97		

I

Iconic	101	Inaccurate packaging terminology	101
'I'm good'	101	Inappropriate Americanisms	102

Inappropriate familiarity	102	Insurance companies	107
Inappropriate use of the present tense	102	Intentional obtuseness	107
Incompetent wine pouring	103	Invitation	108
Ineffective toasters	104	Invite	109
Infantilisation	105	Irish theme pubs	109
Instructions	106		

J

Jeans with slits, tears, rips etc	111

K

Kafka	113	Kids	114
Kafkaesque dealings with remote, cold-hearted, uncomprehending corporate monoliths	113		

L

Lavatory paper discarded at a beauty spot	117	Lightbulbs	120
Law	117	Litter	120
Lazy stereotypes	117	Lived experiences	121
Leggings	118	Long-stay carparks	121
Letting the interests of species like bats, toads and newts trump those of the human race	119		

M

Madrigals	123	Milk in first	126
Male washrooms	123	Mispronunciation of English words on foreign public address systems	128
Mamils	123		
Mansplaining	124		
Manspreading	125	Modern-day child and baby contraptions	128
Maps, on which, wherever you are, you are always on the fold or the edge	125	Morris dancers	130
		Moths	130
Medicine cabinets	126	My truth	131
Menus	126		

N

Name badges	133
Nausea-inducing fried eggs	133
Needing to pee when skiing	134
Nests of tables	135
Net curtains	135
Nibbles	135
No-platforming	137

O

Officialdom	139
Omnipresent yobbishness	139
Ostentatious physical exercises	139
Out-of-reach parking machines	140

P

Painting	143
Painting a fence having taken the trouble to check the weather forecast, only for the heavens to open just as you're finishing	143
Pairing	143
Paninis	144
Paper cuts	144
Pebbledash	144
People who go to fancy dress parties without bothering to wear fancy dress	146
People who seem incapable of following the simplest of instructions	146
People with no taste	147
Perennial unpunctuality	148
Perpetually disrupted picnics	149
Pettifogging rules	149
Picnics	150
Piercings	150
Pillows that do the opposite of what nature intended	151
Plastic bags in supermarkets that want to remain as a single sheet of double-ply plastic rather than allow themselves to open up and serve a useful purpose	152
Plastic netting containers for shop-bought fruit and veg	152
Plugs	152
Pool robots	153
Popular culture	153
Potpourri	154
Printers that prompt suicidal thoughts	154

Q

Queues	157

R

Red ropes outside wannabe in-demand venues	159
Relentless spam emails	159
Removing shoes on a plane	161

Repeat online purchases which are unstoppable	161
Replacement bus service	161
Resto pubs	162

S

Salad on a hot plate	165
Sash windows	165
Secondary glazing	165
Self-assembly furniture	167
Self-important gins	167
Selfish – or should I say, lethal bastard – cyclists	168
Self-tangling wires	168
Serviettes, paper	169
Shared tables on trains	170
She/her and all the other similar abominations	170
Sherry, sweet	171
Signs	171
Singing loudly at concerts	171
Skiing	171
Sleeps	171
Smart motorways	172
Rolling news	162
Roundabouts	163
Rules	163
Smoked salmon packaging	172
Sneezing	172
Snowboards	172
Sofas with bits that tilt	173
Soundtracks in toilets	173
Spam	174
Spanish food	174
Staycations	175
Steak served in a restaurant that bears no relation whatsoever to the style in which you ordered it	176
Stereotypes	177
Stupid car names	177
Super-excited	178
Super-hydration	178
Swear words	179
Sweet sherry	179

T

Tailgating	181
Technology continually making expensive, treasured things redundant	182
Teenage spots when you're middle-aged	183
Textspeak	183
That horrid concrete section of the M25	184
Theatres	184
The bad taste of earlier generations	184
The British three-pin plug	185
The C of E	186
The common cold	187
The 'eco' setting on washing machines and dishwashers	187
The insurance racket	187
The law	188
The near-impossibility of putting children's shoes on	188
The never-ending difficulties with Airfix	189

The Oscars ceremony	189
The perils of painting	190
The person next to you at a gig singing so loudly that you can't actually hear the performer you've paid almost £100 and queued for four hours to see	190
The price of bottled water	191
Therapy	191
The sad decline in the use of proper English swear words	192
The way that French people negotiate roundabouts	193
The wrong (kind of) trousers	194
The wrong regional accents on regional TV stations	195
Things that were once good but have now gone off	195
Thongs	196
Three-pin plugs	197
Toasters	197
Totally over-the-top allergens listings	197
Tradesmen who diss the efforts of their predecessors	197
Trousers	198
Trousers you've just pressed when you realise you've created a 'double-crease'	198
Truculent cabbies	199
Truth	200
TV remote controls	201

U

Unpunctuality	203
Unruly medicine cabinets	203
Unwanted brownfield sites seemingly ripe for development	203
Updating	204
Useless corkscrews	204
Utterly absurdly ridiculously unnecessarily long passwords	205

V

Vending machines that refuse to deliver the goods	209

W

Waiting staff with loud, hyper-energetic movements	211
Waste	212
Water	212
Weeds	212
WFH	213
White wine spritzers	214
Wild madder	214
Wine	214
Wine spillages	214
Wires	215
Workplaces	215
World-class	215

X

X-ray airport staff	217

Y

Yawning	219	Yoghurt	219
Yobbishness	219		

Z

Zeitgeist 221

Acknowledgements 223

Introduction

To those of you who had either the good taste to buy or the good fortune to be given the first volume of *The Becket List* it will come as no surprise that there was no dearth of source material available to fill a second. And to those for whom Volume Two is your first exposure to *The Becket List* you will, after a few moments, no doubt rejoice in the discovery that a First Volume exists.

Of course, with so much BIG STUFF happening in the intervening period (Brexit… Covid… Johnson… Trump… Afghanistan… Ukraine… blah blah blah) there was a temptation to get involved in all this. But good sense prevailed, and the contents of this second book are no less inconsequential than the first. In fact, it's probably safe to say there isn't a single entry of any great moment whatsoever (which is not to say that it doesn't qualify as great literature, self-evidently).

None of which, of course, detracts from its essential purpose, namely to improve the human condition. After all, it is the profoundly irritating, utterly unnoteworthy stuff of daily life that more than anything eats into your soul and makes one question the value of our very existence. Even more than the vagaries of the weather…the awfulness of daytime television…or the incompetence of most bartenders.

The chief aim of this book, therefore, is to underline that YOU ARE NOT ALONE. Other people in the past have suffered – and no doubt generations to come will suffer – the same sort of tribulations that *The Becket List* has identified and to which, in many cases, proffered a solution.

By all means contribute your own thoughts on the matter, by emailing contact@thebecketlist.com, and – who knows – it is entirely possible that enough material will accumulate to merit a third volume.

Absence of worthwhile signs amongst a forest of unnecessary ones

This is a universal affliction, but let me illustrate the point by reference to a hotel guest (we might refer to him as Henry Becket) exiting the Hilton Garden Inn hotel next to Heathrow's Terminal 2, by means of the route that takes him to Terminal 2. In all probability this is at some unearthly hour of the morning (4.30 a.m., since you ask, otherwise why on earth would anyone choose to stay at such a godforsaken location), which means that you will be barely half-awake. But we'll let that pass. Emerging blinking into the neon-lit carpark, having followed signs for 'T2 Walkway' thus far, you will find yourself in an alien landscape of parked cars, and wonder where the **** to head next, all signs save for threatening notices about the direction cars should take having now dematerialised.

With luck and a modicum of intuition, and almost certainly after a few false starts, you will eventually find yourself entering the hallowed grounds of 'The Queen's Terminal 2'. It is a racing certainty that you will want to head for T2 Departures, since that will be your reason for making this sojourn in the first place. But try as you might you will find signs for pretty much everything of note within a five-mile radius of Hounslow – except, of course, 'T2 Departures'. The other terminals get a mention, as do the links to London – which it is quite likely you will have used the day before – and the Chapel (in this diversity-obsessed era now known as the Prayer or Worship Room). And beneath the grotesque multi-million-pound tin sculpture you can glimpse 'Arrivals'. But of 'Departures' you can see no sign (pun intended).

If I were to list all the manifestations of this syndrome that one encounters month by month, this book would be reduced to the literary qualities of a catalogue, so I shall forbear and allow you to make your own mentions in the margins.

Absurdly dramatic yawning in public

Look, I've no doubt that your tonsils are so incredibly gorgeous that wanting to flaunt them frequently is the most natural thing in the world, but seriously – do all the rest of us REALLY have to suffer the sight of them? Worse, do we need to experience the Yogi-Bear-style not-so-sotto-voce growling-type noises that typically accompany the facial contortions of the dramatic public yawner? Not to mention morning breath, the bane of commuters forced to share intimate space with strangers for half an hour first thing in the day. Did no one teach you to position the hand politely in front of your mouth if you genuinely are unable to stifle a yawn in inappropriate circumstances? I'm sure this wasn't an issue a generation ago.

On the other hand, there are, of course, situations in which dramatic yawning in public is to be encouraged, e.g. in the theatre audience at a tediously worthy and woke play; during a concert of anything atonal; or when someone at a dinner party doesn't draw breath whilst telling you how simply amazing their bloody undeserved six-month fully salaried sabbatical was. The key question then – when the speaker asks, 'Sorry, am I boring you?' – is 'Do you have the nerve to answer, "Yup, frankly I haven't heard anything so ball-achingly tedious in the past six months, and that includes the *Shipping Forecast*"?'

Absurdly over-complicated menu descriptions

One of the many great things about Bordeaux, where I've had the good fortune to spend a lot of my life, is that the excellent regional food requires b★★★★r all by way of detailed description. *Plateau de fruits de mer…côte de boeuf…frites…poulet de landes…duck confit* – I could go on (and almost inevitably will). Not for the Bordelais the flowery OTT menu listings so beloved of affected establishments around the world.

The same, of course, goes for wine, but that's ground I've covered in the first volume (thinly disguised sales pitch, obvs)…

See also Allergies

'Accessible Toilets'

Please tell me – what is the point of any other kind?

Adults with 'sippy cups'/neo baby bottles

Just grow up! Even the beaker folk tens of thousands of years ago were sufficiently developed to have mastered the art of drinking from something that was recognisably a mug. Even in their primitive state they didn't require a spout/teat/sucker to ingest liquid, so why now have so many supposedly advanced peoples regressed so much? If you're midway through the Tour de France weaving your way up the Col du Tourmalet, for example, or halfway down a black run in Val d'Isère, I see why a delicate piece of bone china might be slightly impractical – especially the accompanying saucer – but if you're sitting at a desk in Homerton?! Or on the 17.49 from Waterloo?! Jeez.

Affecting to be something/someone you're not

A couple of generations ago it was comical to detect the products of elocution classes (a little like Patricia Routledge playing Hyacinth Bucket – sorry, *Bouquet* – in *Keeping Up Appearances*), trying so hard to be something they self-evidently were not. But for years now, of course, it has been fashionable to affect a different kind of 'social mobility', for want of a neater phrase. Estuary English has perhaps been its most notorious manifestation, with the obligatory use of the ugly glottal (should that be glo'al?) stop, and refusal to pronounce the g in words ending in ing, preferring instead the apostrophe closure now mandatory throughout popular discourse – including you, Mrs Home Secretary at the time of writing. You also hear a different kind of affectation from people who want to appear 'street' as I believe it is known and who speak what has been described as 'Jafaican' – a Caribbean patois beloved of Home Counties housing estates.

Age-inappropriate clothing

I have more than once been berated for wearing what 'management' refer to as 'the inappropriate trousers', by which she means my favourite battered pair of low-rise off-white Diesels with more zips in more places than anyone could need. But putting my questionable foibles to one side, there is no question that the old adage of 'mutton dressed as lamb' is generally a good rule to live by. Minuscule bikinis on matrons are not a good look; T-shirts with unfunny drug-related slogans don't work on middle-aged city-boys; muffin tops don't befit crop tops; and so on.

The same goes for elderly women sporting spindly stilettos and fascinators (presumably an ironic term, incidentally, in view of their sheer ghastliness), and at the other extreme, twenty-year-olds fresh from some minor public school clad in cherry-red cords and a panama, for all the world like a retired half-colonel. Infinitely worse, of course, is a tween in a uniform more appropriate to a low-grade hooker, and anyone over forty trudging wearily through a shopping centre in sports gear. On which note, it is a truism that almost every bloke wearing a replica football shirt looks unlikely to be able to WALK the length of a football pitch – let alone run around one.

Airfix

See The never-ending difficulties with Airfix

Airport shops

Why? Airports are for getting on or off a plane. If you want to go to a shop – go to the shops. What makes it worse is how they create longer routes to get from A to B to make sure that you go past ALL the shops. The newest development – clearly the outcome of a massive management consultancy project – is to create vast maze-like structures with no easily identifiable exit, and in which thousands of people mill about aimlessly, buying unwanted things in the desperate hope that maybe by purchasing something they'll magically be given the key that unlocks the door and lets them out. They're the ones you hear about on the public address system ('This flight is ready to depart: if Mr and Mrs Grot and their ghastly children do not arrive within eight seconds, their luggage will be offloaded and you will not be permitted to depart today').

Then there's the fantasy that they're charging 'better than High Street prices'. And 'everyone pays duty-free prices'. Yeah, right. And who wants to spend half a week's salary on a giant Toblerone anyway, or a bright pink canister of aftershave, or an unheard-of whisky named something like 'Caber Tosser's ten-year-old Deluxe Double-Blended Suspiciously Orange-coloured Genuine Scotch Whisky'?

See also Having to show your boarding card at airport shops

Air travel

Time was, not so long ago, when air travel was borderline glamorous – and I don't just mean for those who could afford to shell out for transatlantic trips on Concorde. Even airports, back in the day, had the air of places where not EVERYONE was admitted. Now, of course, the situation has been reversed, to the extent that the majority of the people you will try not to bump into are EXACTLY the kind of people you try to avoid bumping into as you go about your daily business. But setting that – and the awfulness of air travel in the Covid era – aside, has anyone (by which I suppose I mean 'managers' of airports and airlines) apart from seasoned travellers registered the gruesome decline in standards in the past decade or so? It is, for example, something of an 'event' when an encounter with officialdom is anything other than exasperating. Sometimes it is for all the world as if you're back standing outside the Deputy Head's office in the late sixties, gritting your teeth and awaiting your punishment for some minor infringement of some fatuous rule that you didn't even know existed.

And the QUEUING! It is invariably endless, with interminable shuffling around a series of maze-like zigzags and chicanes that keep kidding you that you're 'almost there'. And the pettifogging rules about luggage – and the continuous stream of announcements over the Tannoy, almost without exception stating and restating the bleeding obvious. And once you're aboard, the unending loudspeaker instructions continue, saying the same thing that you – and no doubt pretty much everyone else – has heard several million times before, with the net result that they have all the usefulness of a chocolate teapot. The job of an air hostess, naturally, these days has all the appeal of a bus conductress on the roughest of nightbus routes, which no doubt largely explains the recruitment policies of most airlines.

Alcohol content of wine

Time was, when the extravagant alcohol content of the Lebanon's Château Musar was a thing of rare wonderment. When most wines were a gentle 11–12%, Musar's 17% was something to be savoured and shown off. But now even the meanest of reds seem to boast figures like 14% – and you'll even get whites dished up with a strength redolent of the roughest grappa. What this means, of course, is that half a bottle down and you're already half-p****d and ready for a nap. The trade blames hotter climates and the desperation of much of the public to get smashed at every opportunity, a trend compounded by the omnipresence of extra large glasses, where a previous generation believed a 125ml glass to be a tad on the generous side. Give me a large glass containing a small amount of very good quality wine every time, refilled as necessary, rather than one of the buckets of questionable-quality quaffing wine that seem to be de rigueur.

Ale in cans

Why is it that something perfectly inoffensive like Old Rector's Todger can be moderately enjoyable pulled in a pub but thoroughly objectionable from a can? It's not just aesthetic considerations (though this doesn't help, obviously) but some reaction must take place between the surface of the can and its contents to render a normally cleansing ale utterly undrinkable.

And doesn't the same happen to orange juice – but not, for example, to tonic water? This is one of life's most impenetrable conundrums, the only response to which is to avert one's gaze when walking down the aisle of a supermarket that contains such banalities, and contemplate higher things – such as the relative proximity of the Hope and Anchor with its line of guest ales, and the thought that you might be there in a matter of minutes.

Alexa

Apart from the fun to be had asking 'her' to pronounce a hundred in Welsh (don't tell me you haven't tried it) or inviting 'her' to regale you with her impressive portfolio of flatulence sound-effects, Alexa is manifestly one of the abominations of the age. And apparently she's listening, ever-eager, to all the drivel that pervades your otherwise entirely normal household. Best avoided.

Allergies

How is it POSSIBLE that the majority of the UK population now suffer from a host of allergies that I'm not sure even existed a generation ago? Why is every flight I take thronged with people who are going to die a horrific instantaneous death if someone within twenty rows so much as opens a packet of dry-roasted peanuts? Why are waiting staff in restaurants seemingly more interested in your list of allergies than taking your order? I could go on (and in all likelihood will).

Not long ago I was presented with a breakfast menu in which every single item was encoded as if it were part of a wartime entry exam for Hut 14 at Bletchley Park. Here is a snapshot of the rubric at the bottom:

V = suitable for vegetarians;

VE = suitable for vegans;

VE★ = dish can be amended to be suitable for vegans;

G = gluten;

C = crustaceans (at BREAKFAST, for pity's sake?!);

E = eggs;

F = fish;

M = molluscs (served at a snail's pace…fair enough, that's something to which I AM allergic);

S= soybeans/soya;

P = peanuts;

N = nuts (yep, you are);

MK = milk/dairy (but not, oddly enough, Milton Keynes, to which I have an intolerance bordering on fatal);

CY = celery;

MD = mustard;

SS = sesame seeds;

SP = sulphites;

L = Lupins.

And as if this wasn't insane enough – I don't actually have any allergies I know of since you ask, apart from to inanity – having taken so much pseudo-care for the welfare of its customers, this benighted, hideously expensive establishment produced a full English breakfast that, whilst it looked realistic, was STONE COLD. Why wasn't this flagged with an SC, I hear you ask? I'd have done better at one of those totally unpretentious roadside truck-stops that flies a Union Flag – AND avoided interrogation regarding my health non-issues.

Americanisms

See Inappropriate Americanisms

Apologising for no reason

Having discussed this numerous times, I'm aware that this syndrome doesn't only inflict me. So what IS it that makes so many of us apologise when no apology is due? I'm talking about moments like when someone's barged into you on the pavement, and yet inevitably you're the one who says, 'Oops, sorry' – a word which is clearly not in their vocabulary, and which in any case is wasted on them on account of them being plugged into their headphones, oblivious to all around them. It happens in pubs, restaurants, trains, planes…pretty much everywhere, in fact. For once, I'm at a loss to explain it and have tried to stop, but there's an inbuilt mechanism – presumably imbibed with breast milk from my good-manners-obsessed mother – that makes this impossible. And trust me, I'm not invariably the politest person around…

See also Fellow guests on the lookout for someone more interesting

Apple

The fruit is perfectly OK (though many would aver, nothing like as tasty as decades ago; someone please tell me why), but the corporation absolutely is not. Self-satisfied, smug, over-large and overly in control of its devices even when you — the purchaser — have taken up ownership. And why is it all so complicated — e.g. illegibly small serial numbers, impossible-to-open SIM card apertures – and NEVER a decent set of instructions to guide you?

Arndale Centres

Arnold Hagenbach and Sam Chippindale have a lot to answer for. Starting in Jarrow in 1961 they started a trend in this land of once-bustling high streets that has blighted the country. Has ANYONE ever enjoyed a visit to an Arndale Centre? If so, it has to be assumed that all their sensory abilities were surgically removed prior to disembarking from the number 37 in the contiguous – or worse, integral – bus station. Half-full of charity shops, pound shops and the naffest type of chain stores, the phrase 'Abandon Hope, All Ye Who Enter Here' might have been devised as the Arndale Centre's mission statement. It is, I suppose, just possible that Jeff Bezos had the idea of killing off these gruesome edifices in mind when he first came up with the concept of Amazon, so maybe some good will come of it, though sadly the effects are rather indiscriminate, in the process exterminating half of all the worthy little shops that still linger on our benighted high streets.

'Around…'

As in, for example, 'we're talking around the issue of…', as spoken by a pretentious broadcaster. Where did this absurd new usage of a perfectly satisfactory word creep up from? How come 'about' is suddenly redundant? On a related subject, did you know that in the States, according to your rented satnav, you don't approach a roundabout, but 'a traffic circle'? Ridiculous. But I suppose that at least that's better than France, where the chances of your actually approaching a *rond point* is close to zero, given that the French have yet to master the art of navigating around one...

See also The way that French people negotiate roundabouts

Assumptive form-filling rubrics

Just because the form that you are required to complete online or your satnav destinations feature has been devised by some *urbanista* based in the world's greatest conurbation on America's West Coast, doesn't mean that ALL of us live in a 'city'. Neither Nether Wallop nor Chenac Saint Seurin d'Uzet, the two places I happen to inhabit, qualify as such, so I'd be grateful if a more appropriate descriptor could be provided. Thank you.

Au pairs

Can be easy on the eye and therefore an occasionally welcome distraction from the realities of everyday domestic life, but that attribute aside, almost always entirely useless. Especially if hired with the express purpose of sharing the burden of child-rearing, at which they will be predictably hopeless; or doing the school run, whereupon you discover on arrival that they've already written off three cars back home. Clearly, if not easy on the eye, it is difficult to see the point of an au pair at all.

Auto responses to email

I can't be the only person who resents the impudence of things like Gmail, that have the audacity to presume how I might wish to reply to a communication. Look, the thingy you sent me was… all right…fine…acceptable, sure. It might even be really quite good. I do not, however, wish to exclaim 'Love it!', 'Brilliant!', 'Very fun!' (seriously) or some such. I yearn for the plodding pedestrianism of a quieter era, when I – or to be fair, more likely my long-suffering secretary – would reply along the lines of, 'I am in receipt of your letter and its enclosures of the xth and will revert at my earliest convenience'. And while I'm at it, don't you hanker after the days of secretaries and the endless scope not just for inappropriate behaviour but innocent amusement occasioned by mistakes that were only marginally important? My favourite concerns the letter to a diminutive client from a friend of mine, whose secretary concluded a letter with the immortal phrase, 'I look forwards to seeing you again shorty'. Happy days.

Awaydays

Once a term for a British Rail ticket offer, more frequently used these days in the context of poor excuses to empty the office building of a lot of people who would otherwise be gainfully employed. Although not necessarily, in both senses: awaydays have been known to be held ON-SITE, and a lot of the people attending were probably not gainfully employed in the first place. In the days before casual wear became de rigueur throughout the world of commerce, it was also an excuse for colleagues who only ever see each other in fairly sensible clothes to turn up in mufti – the more age-inappropriate, the better.

B

'Back to School'

A retail/online promotion that invariably commences at the very start of the longest holiday of the school year, thus inducing palpitations in school attendees of a nervous disposition and a sense of doom amongst those parents who for the first time in a year have to cope with the continuous presence of their offspring.

On shop windows and in ads, the words are almost always printed in a childlike font, gaily coloured, with at least one of the letters written – one hopes with a sense of irony – backwards. How witty! The irony is sometimes unintentionally enhanced by the device of spelling school as SKOOL (and back as BAKC), the last resort of the desperate Mac artworker (but probably at the behest of the under junior marketer, straight from some media course). All such promotions are to be ignored, in the hope that one day they will cease to exist, but seeing as they are near-universal (you will find their equivalents throughout Europe, though probably not in Italy where any hint of 'work' is obviously wildly inappropriate), this is probably a lost cause.

Backwards baseball caps

No one has ever been able to explain to me why – if a baseball cap has to be worn at all – it should be worn backwards. It is surprising that no one has invented a cap with the peak sewn onto the reverse, but maybe that is just too obvious. It is perfectly understandable that those chaps in the Eighth Army fighting against Rommel in North Africa chose to wear those hats with the bit of cloth protecting the back of your neck from the noonday sun, but is it really necessary at the Emirates Stadium on a damp December evening? And what is it with those Formula One drivers and those bizarre baseball-type caps with the over-extended peak and weird extra height? Since they're all only about five foot six to start with, I guess it must be to put them up there with the rappers. Guys – it doesn't work, take it from me. You might as well have lifts in your shoes.

Bad coffee

Setting aside the obvious category of bad coffee that is 'instant coffee' (*see* Vol. I), I cannot bear the pretence of good coffee that is too often the experience in an establishment that no doubt thinks of itself as upscale. How many times are you presented with a small puddle of acrid deep brown liquid that barely covers the bottom of a large cup that the server has the gall to explain is a single espresso? In a vessel that is so cold it might have languished in the freezer overnight. And almost inevitably the lump of sugar you are expected to use will be of a larger surface area than the coffee itself, which means that you have no choice but to wrestle two thirds of the lump out in a semi-molten mass to watch it slowly disintegrate in the saucer.

Mysteriously, when you foolishly order a second from the assistant – who no doubt rejoices in the invariably inappropriate descriptor 'barista' – but to ring the changes ask for a double espresso, what arrives is identical in quantity to the single you just gulped down in a single unenjoyable mouthful. What's THAT about?!

See also Barista

Badly made spritzers

The next time a barman shoves a white wine spritzer in my direction that contains any of the following, I swear I'll chuck it straight back at him: poor quality white wine (one suspects, sometimes, a collection of the dregs from various near-finished bottles that have accumulated over the past several days); lemonade; flat water; a chunk of lemon; and five times as much water as wine. Seriously, I've experienced ALL of those – sometimes simultaneously. A proper spritzer could not be simpler to serve: two measures of decent, dry, cold, freshly opened white wine; one measure of soda water; and a little ice. Er, that's it. The notion that you can use up naff wine in a spritzer in the same way that some use corked redders to make mulled wine or a boeuf bourguignon is utterly misguided. A bit like the old saw relating to computers: rubbish in, rubbish out.

Badly packaged bacon...prosciutto...salami...etc

Surely the machines that pack and seal these products could be instructed to do it PROPERLY?! After seemingly hours of tedious picking away at that little corner of plastic which is supposed to make opening the package easy, it eventually gives way and reveals that it's in entirely the wrong place. All the meat slices are layered in such a way that you now need to remove ALL the plastic to get to the slices that are on top, because they're laid out that way, which inevitably means you have to resort to clingfilm to make good once you've removed the couple of slivers which is all you want. Aaaarrrgghhhh! (*See* Vol. I re clingfilm)

See also Smoked salmon packaging

Bad manners

A scourge of our age, up there with SUVs in suburbia and – oh, come to think of it, just about everything in this list. 'Manners makyth man', or so it used to be believed, but now the opposite seems to be the creed of many people. Almost a badge of honour for some, and one nowadays worn with pride, not a decent sense of inferiority, and passed down the generations. Is it awarded at some rite of passage, it is interesting to speculate – say during the first visit to a fast-food outlet or a theme park – or much earlier, maybe, at some ghastly birthing ceremony? 'Ooh look, he's got his father's shocking manners!' people will likely coo over the baby buggy, as little Zak peers back at you malevolently. *Quelle surprise*.

Bad menu translations

I have to be honest and say, that whilst incompetent menus are unquestionably up there in the pantheon of First World problems, it would take a diner of Scrooge-level meanness of spirit not to delight in some of the funnier examples of mistranslations. Speaking personally, I loved the idea of 'Crudities of the season', which presumably prohibits the use of certain swear words in certain months of the year. 'Foie gras and his toasts' has long been a perennial favourite, in every sense. And it so happens that the waitress who once handed us a menu bearing the word 'sweatness' was exceptionally hot. Oh, how we laughed. Conversely, I was less enamoured of the 'puke bowl' on offer at an Oriental restaurant, and it is inevitably Chinese places that have the greatest potential for slapstick. 'Ice-cream in the ass', 'Fuck the duck until exploded' have been reported, as have such delights as 'Sweet tight pussy' and 'Husband and wife lung slice'. But my first prize goes to a caption under a picture in a takeaway, simply described as 'whatever', which kind of sums up the sector.

See also Absurdly over-complicated menu descriptions, Allergies

Bad spelling etc

How can it be that something that was once completely unacceptable is now almost approved of, in the same way that non-RP accents are now seemingly de rigueur? After all, it's not as if everyone who has their own 'take' on spelling, grammar and punctuation is on the road to be the next James Joyce. It sometimes seems that our long-strived-for civilisation is being dismantled in front of our eyes, brick by brick, misplaced apostrophe by inappropriate comma.

Bad taste

See The bad taste of earlier generations

Barista

Exotic job description given by way of compensation to someone who's flunked their A-levels (or equivalent in any country around the world) and is near-unemployable but finds a role working in a branch of any international chain of coffee shop. Known for their utter incomprehension of the English language (like a Bulgarian working in an English country pub for whom the phrase 'A pint of Best, please' is naturally completely unintelligible), they are programmed only to respond to obscure phrases like, 'Can I get a tall skinny latte made with old vine Colombian arabica and almond milk, not too hot, with a dusting of Moroccan organic 83 per cent chocolate powder' and never a simple request such as, 'A cup of black coffee please.'

See also Bad coffee, 'Can I get…?'

Baseball caps

See Backwards baseball caps

Bathrooms

Necessary and can be very civilised. The usage of this word to describe a toilet/bog/loo/WC/lavatory is thoroughly affected, however (as in, 'Excuse me, where are the bathrooms?'), and not to be tolerated on either side of the Atlantic. Esp. this side.

Being told what to do by your car

Being of a certain age, I still abide by the no doubt antiquated dictum that the DRIVER is in charge of what's going on – not the vehicle. But increasingly I find that this is simply not the case. It all started decades ago when the Volvo I owned (yes, I *should* have known better) took it into its head that the no doubt weighty briefcase beside me on the passenger seat needed to fasten its seat belt: if it didn't, as punishment for disobeying some obscure but doubtless worthy Swedish law of responsible living, it would start a riot of flashing lights and clacking noises until the otherwise unobjectionable briefcase fell into line. But in this era, the rule of the car has been taken to a whole new level. I'm now more or less inured to the instruction to 'take a break' or the warning that I've strayed (intentionally, natch) over the white line, but recently a hire car I was driving repeatedly hectored me to keep my hands on the steering wheel. What is THAT about?! Oh, and they were, obvs.

Best practice

An unintentionally ironic phrase – and as like as not misspelled – much favoured by advisers on business improvement methods. What it SHOULD mean, is the common-sense adoption across a business of an activity that has fortuitously been found to improve results in one part of the company. What it invariably means in actuality is the conscious spreading of a technique – or 'management tool' as, to my mind at least, it is amusingly and appropriately termed – that is as like or not totally fatuous, by a middle manager desperate to earn brownie points for his brown-nosing. Once spread in this way, it of course becomes the exact opposite of best practice – a set-in-concrete aspect of corporate behaviour that is impossible to dislodge and ends up extinguishing every junior manager's last vital spark of entrepreneurialism.

See also Chocolates on pillows, Soundtracks in toilets

Birds relieving themselves on your just-cleaned car

How do they KNOW?!

Birmingham

Should you require a supporting statement, simply ask yourself: Why has no call centre ever been based there?

Bloody car drivers who sneak up on your inside before pulling into the sensible gap you'd left behind the car in front

I'm not generally known for being ultra-sensible, but I do try to leave a reasonable space between my radiator grill and the rear bumper of someone in front going at 70 mph plus – only because I quite like my no-claims bonus and the shape of my bonnet as it is. So I get really cheesed off (that's one way of putting it) when some aggressive little tosser (aren't they always?) takes a fancy to my gap, so to speak, and decides to fill it with his vile little 'hot hatch'. Suddenly, the sensible gap is no more and I have to slam on my brakes – risking the untimely and unwelcome arrival in my boot of the car behind – to give the wretch the requisite room. And then, you know what, he will likely have the temerity to make a series of vulgar remonstrations in response to my perfectly justified gestures of displeasure, before dipping back into the inside lane and performing exactly the same manoeuvre with the car in front that I'd been happily following at a respectable distance for several miles. Grrrrrrr.

Blush wine

No. It's ROSÉ wine. With an acute accent. Blush is an artificial confection, created by marketing types, to attract 'light wine-drinkers'. To be avoided, in the same way as earlier generations learned to give a wide berth to a chemical known as 'Hirondelle'. May be poisonous. The artificially bright pinkness of the liquid is a giveaway (Windolene, anyone?). Even very pale rosé – the type typically favoured by 'ladies who lunch' – is preferable to this.

Books

See Technology continually making expensive, treasured things redundant

Bottled water

See The price of bottled water

Bowties

See Fake bowties

Bum cracks

See Exposed bum cracks

C

Cackling

Why have so many people seemingly given up on the pleasant sound of gentle laughter, in favour of a far coarser means of denoting amusement, to whit – loud cackling? And at the risk of being sexist, why is such a huge proportion of cacklers female? It's the soundtrack of a thousand hen parties, but it's strayed into everyday life. Maybe just about understandable at a stand-up comedy gig, but in a restaurant…a train…an art gallery?!

And why do audiences on faintly humorous radio programmes whoop-whoop and scream in orgiastic delight at the moderately amusing bons mots of the participants – or even their appearance at the start of an episode – when some polite, restrained applause would surely suffice. Or do producers source audience ecstasy from a genuinely funny programme and overlay it onto the mild approbation of the one they've just made?

Call centres

Is there anything in the world to match the sense of helplessness that overcomes one at the start of a 'journey' through a call centre? From the moment you dial the number you already know that it's a lost cause, but still you persist through the menu of options, thinking, 'This time it'll be different', as you press a series of numbers and that hash one. Like as not, at the end of a half-hour process it'll ask you to punch in the one piece of information that you don't have to hand, at which point it will, inevitably, reject you. You know your mother's maiden name… your date of birth…your credit card number…your address…your special date…your account number…the make of your first car/name of first pet/first girlfriend's favourite knickers' colour…even your inside-leg measurement, but still the disembodied voice wants to know something even more obscure.

It's at this point that, having failed the entrance exam, you are instructed to hold the line and an operator will attend to you. You're in a queue…position number eighteen…we're experiencing an unusual level of calls today (yep, what's new). Have you tried our website? (OF COURSE I have! It was useless, which is why I'm trying to talk to a human being). Eventually, by which time your handset is red-hot through continued overuse, the phone gets answered. You're then halfway through pleading, 'PLEASE make a note of my number in case we get cut off' when – guess what? – the call abruptly ends. In my experience the worst offenders are what used to be known – by themselves, natch – as the world's favourite airline, the country's biggest mortgage provider, and Europe's leading mobile phone company.

And then, having failed abysmally to treat you as a valued customer – or indeed as human being – they have the NERVE to follow up with a text asking you to rate their service (your opinion is important to us…we're always trying to improve our service… LIARS).

Aaaaaaaarrrrrgggggghhhhhhhhhh!!!!!

Cancel culture

Not so long ago, my alma mater, for centuries in the vanguard of liberal, rational, enlightened thinking, got into a spot of bother about a stained-glass window which commemorated a chap who had been both rather brilliant and the holder, it turns out, of somewhat distasteful ideas about people (eugenics, say no more). In the ensuing kerfuffle, it seems that in all likelihood the window will be removed, as a statement that 'we don't hold with that sort of thing'. Forgetting the whys and wherefores of this particular episode, the key question, of course, is… Where will it all end? A relatively recent and much-revered master of the same institution, whose portrait hangs in the hall, rather more prominently than the aforementioned stained-glass window, was an infamous apologist for perhaps history's greatest mass murderer, one Chairman Mao. Is he also to be banished to the backstairs of the undercroft? And at the time of writing, England's finest cathedrals are undertaking an audit of the statuary which abound in their establishments, with a view to deciding who should get the chop, in the wake – one hopes not literally – of the Colston statue which ended up in Bristol docks.

Given the timidity and wokefulness of the new generation, I suppose a little plaque giving a more nuanced potted history of the chap (it's almost always a chap) being memorialised is justifiable, in the same way as the wretched National Trust now plans to explain how some eighteenth-century family came by its wealth, so often partly by nefarious means: I ask you, how many people over the centuries have accumulated enormous wealth entirely by admirable means? This is on a par with us having to apologise for the sins of earlier generations. After decades of having been rightly adjured not to blame contemporary Germans for the ghastliness of the Nazis, it's a bit rich for you and I to have to grovel about what our forebears did in drawing up the lines of demarcation between Syria and Iraq, for example; the Indian Partition; or imposing lethal reparations on post-Great War Germany. Enough questionable stuff is done in our name right now, without having to be continuously abasing ourselves for stuff carried out generations before.

See also Content warnings, No-platforming, National Trust (Vol. I)

Candles in jars that stop working when they're a quarter of the way through

So you're confronted by a jar in which sits a candle, which no doubt as a result probably cost five times what the candle alone would have cost.

To start with, all seems pleasing – if you like that kind of thing. Then, a few evenings in, you find that the wick has all but disappeared and the damn thing won't ignite. You try the upside-down thing, lighting it, as it were, from beneath, to no avail. All you get is hot wax on your hands and in all probability on some frighteningly pristine surface below. Next, flying in the face of decades of – how do I put it – negative experiences, you attempt to excavate the solid wax around where you're sure the wick is embedded. Starting off with a teaspoon then resorting to the sharpest knife in the kitchen drawer, after ten minutes you eventually expose a few paltry millimetres of wick. Wahay! Progress! One more dig and… dammit!…You've now given it the most brutal of circumcisions – or more accurately, the whole Bobbitt. The end has disappeared, and all chance of it ever again being lit have gone. Memo to self: next time one of those candle-in-a-fancy-jar contrivances suffers an early demise, just bin it before you lose the will to live. I ask you, is it any wonder that so many candles-in-a-jar are regifted?

'Can I get…?'

Setting aside for the moment the solecism which led the questioner to ask such a tautological question (there is little doubt in most circumstances that the person speaking would be physically able to get the item in question), there is a deeper absurdity. If you're confronting a barman or a barista (God help you with THAT one!), surely the question is simply, 'Please may I have a…?' In the circumstances, it is self-evidently the respondent's job to 'get' whatever is being requested. QED.

See also Barista

Car names

See Stupid car names

Car rear-ends

Why is that all current-day cars have such utterly hideous rear-ends? How I miss the elegance of a sixties Cadillac Eldorado or even the more modest Singer Gazelle! The framed prints of bygone eras often found on pub walls provide ample evidence of what an aesthetic deficit we now suffer, with cars' backsides these days too often an unfortunate collection of mismatched angles, light clusters, indentations and fussy ill-thought-through detailing. Is it any wonder that the ads for one of the few cars launched in recent times possessing a distinctive, characterful, stylish bottom majored on this distinguishing feature: 'I see ya baby, shakin' that ass!' went the refrain, celebrating the looks of the then-new Renault Megane – and quite right too.

See also Exposed bum cracks

Chains of coffee shops

Starbucks, Costa, Caffè Nero etc ad almost infinitum. Indisputably, and without exception, to be avoided at all costs, on account of their omnipresence; 'fake barista culture'; often atrocious attitudes to corporate responsibility; general joylessness; strange division of labour between order-takers, coffee-makers, servers and payment-takers; horrid sofas; and hordes of 'consultants' 'hotdesking' there for hours on end. Oh – and mostly vile coffee, too, obviously.

See also Barista, Bad coffee, 'Can I get…?'

Children kicking the back of your seat on a flight

Why does this activity give children a degree of pleasure out of all proportion to the amount of talent and preparation it requires? More than that, why do their parents so often see it as inoffensive – charming, even – when you can bet your bottom (pun intended) dollar that, sitting where you are, they'd find the experience more akin to the form of medieval torture allegedly suffered by, among others, King Edward II. But in his case, not the entire duration of a flight to Florida.

Children's shoes

See The near-impossibility of putting shoes on children

Chilled ale

As any fule kno (prop. Molesworth, N.), ale should be served at the temperature at which it emerges from the cellar. Blood temperature is also obviously wrong, but not as wrong as COLD. If you actually notice your chosen tipple making its way via your mouth, gullet and stomach on its way to the inevitable exit – trust me, it's the WRONG TEMPERATURE. Ale should gently slide down, without making a song and dance about it. Er, that's it. Simple really: no need to be bitter.

Chocolates on pillows

Yes, yes, I know this has been written about before. Indeed, a whole book has been written about what they symbolise. But we've still failed to get this abysmal hotel practice stamped out. And no – it's not enough merely to substitute a couple of pathetically small boiled sweets in wrappers in their place. Why not substitute an appropriate nightcap (no – not THAT kind, obvs)?

See also Best practice, Soundtracks in toilets

Christmas tree lights

Why, oh why do I ever think that last year's string of Christmas lights will still work? It must be the innate optimist in me, as readers of this and an earlier volume will have come to well understand. But in truth a sense of foreboding fills me as soon as I open the box. I know with absolute certainty that either it won't work at all – or worse, that it'll kid you it's working, and then go on to fail within minutes of the tree being decorated, and hours of work are now called for to disentangle the whole bloody lot, in the course of which you will of course smash at least one of the family's most precious baubles and destroy any possibility of a congenial pre-Christmas ambience for at least forty-eight hours.

Talking of which, how is it that, however carefully you packed last year's lights away, it inevitably takes a couple of hours, a lot of swearing and a stiff whisky to unpick the cat's cradle of wires and bulbs before you can think about reusing them?

And finally: MUST they flash? Less is more, as someone much more deeply philosophical than me once observed.

Cider

Nothing wrong with an apple – well, some apples. And absolutely nothing wrong with a decent drop of Calvados. But who in their right mind would want to sluice down a cider? Mr orchard-keeper, kindly put your apples to good use and dish up a nice tarte Tatin, an apple and blackberry crumble or a tarte aux pommes and don't try to kid us that cider is like ale, only fruitier. It's just – not. There is the possibly (possibly not?) apocryphal tale of the visitor to Somerset who sampled a local cider in a pub. When he asked where it was made, he was told – on the premises. 'Well, it doesn't travel very well,' he replied. Believe me – none does. And as for that Magners – the less said, the better.

Clinking glasses

Until very recently it was enough simply to raise one's glass in a gesture that said 'Cheers', perhaps accompanied by the uncomplicated word, 'Cheers'. Maybe even with the addition of an exclamation mark. But no longer. Where did this notion of having to clink glasses every time yours gets refilled spring up from – and why? And why do you have to do it every time you move on from G and T to white to red to brandy? And why, for pity's sake, do you have to do that weird thing of making eye contact with everyone involved (on pain of a bollocking if you don't) for all the world as if you're lighting the cigarette of a girl back in the seventies and don't want to bring bad luck? Who invents these rules?!

Clothes on animals

Absurd, fatuous and fetishistic, with apologies for the near-tautology. If the animal is cold, keep it indoors, for pity's sake – don't doll it up in doll's type clothing! And as for dogs in handbags…

You can make a case for a horse-blanket, or one of those hoods for horses' heads that keep flies at bay, or even the ridiculously twee culottes worn by some French donkeys in a previous age (*L'Ane Culotte*, I'm not making this up), allegedly to keep sandflies at bay but more likely in the manner of Victorians disguising a shapely table-leg with a few yards of broderie anglaise lest the onlooker gets aroused. The Welsh have sheep, the French have – well pretty much anything, one suspects.

C of E

See The C of E

Coffee bores and incompetents

Some years ago, at a motorway service station way oop north, one of my travelling companions, unsure as to the quality of the caff, asked of the 'barista', 'What's your cappuccino like?' Back came the immortal answer in a strong Yorkshire accent in an unintentionally withering put-down: 'It's a frothy coffee.'

Unwittingly, our man had hit on an important truth: most coffee orders beyond the simplest are of course total bollocks.

'I'll have a decaffeinated, low fat, extra-hot vanilla latte – oh and make it with foam on top would you?' and other such nonsense demands are what make the queues at typical coffee shops so unbearable. Absurdities such as soy milk, coconut milk, sprinkles of God knows what, extra shots, half-shots, flavourings, drizzles and the like have escaped from their natural habitat – America's West Coast – and taken root in provincial England, when really all you need to state is black or white, oh, and ask where the sugar can be found. Did our forebears really go through shortages and rationing in the forties and fifties just so that the woke generation can make such priceless fools of themselves? And, of course, the irony of butting in and advising this finicky lot to 'wake up and smell the coffee' would be utterly lost on them.

Which is not to say that some specifics aren't vital when it comes to coffee ordering or after-the-event complaining. Old man Illy who died at an advanced age not long ago was rightly famous for his fastidiousness when it came to the important details: the right beans, roasted at the right temperature for the requisite time, freshly ground, served from a routinely cleaned machine filled with good quality water, etc etc. But sadly, far too many incompetents don't get even these right and then go on to serve a minute, tepid *ristretto* that barely covers the bottom of a cold chunky mug with a chip in the lip and costs you north of a fiver. One suspects that even a dollop of ersatz chicory 'coffee' from an enamel mug in the bombed-out ruins of Berlin would sometimes be a preferable experience…

See also Bad coffee, Barista

Coffee shops

See Chains of coffee shops

Cohort

When Covid is finally over, please can this overused word be rested for a few centuries?

Cold blocks in the freezer that are itching to jump out

Is it possible that the world's most super-slippery product has already been invented, and is just idling there under our noses in the freezer compartment, waiting to be discovered and make trillions for the first person to realise its potential, like the man who invented those wire cages which contain stones? I refer, of course, to those little blue cold blocks that we take on picnics, which are incapable of staying put whenever one reaches for the ice tray in readiness for the next G and T, jettisoning themselves in an absurdly dramatic fashion, for all the world like a *Star Wars* escape pod. I am surely not the only person who is forever picking them off the kitchen floor in their frozen state, at which point they so securely fasten themselves to one's hands that you begin to fear for the structural integrity of the epidermis?

Cold potatoes

Surely no one sane doubts that the only good potato is a hot potato (Spanish restaurants and salad-makers, please note)? These can be boiled, roasted, chipped, sautéed, fried, deep-fried, triple-fried (best of all, preferably in antique duck fat) etc but NEVER served cold. It's not how God intended them to be enjoyed (ask Sir Walter Raleigh).

The same, naturally, applies to rice and pasta. Both take on the texture of something more akin to wallpaper paste/India rubber when served cold. Very nasty.

Collagen

Undeniably useful – one should perhaps say essential, given its role in the make-up of mammals – in its natural state, but equally, undeniably awful as a treatment or supplement. What on earth is wrong with the odd wrinkle or laughter line, for goodness' sake – and what on earth is RIGHT with a taut, expressionless face, seemingly incapable of any kind of movement? Never was the phrase 'Go on, crack a smile!' more apt than in relation to someone whose face has been stuffed so full of collagen that it looks in danger of disintegrating if the wind changes... I give you the infamous 'bride of Wildenstein' as evidence for the prosecution.

Commentators

See Great sportsmen who are subsequently inappropriately hired as commentators

Committees

A well-intentioned organisational device conceived with the intention of making things happen, but which almost invariably has the exact opposite effect. 'May I speak through the chair?' 'I have the floor.' Oh, please. What a load of nonsense. Forget the committee-speak, get out of the committee-room and go and get something actually done, Mr Deputy Chair. Or more likely, set up a sub-committee that will do even less, over more time, and be even more smug about it – because they're SPECIAL.

Common cold

See The common cold

Complicated door handles

In a happy, not long-departed era, one could approach a door – pretty much any door – in the confident expectation that one would be able to open or close it. That, after all, is the primary function of a door, and it would seem sensible for it to be constructed in such a way that most self-respecting adults would be capable of this most basic of actions.

So what is it these days with these complicated contraptions whose role in life seems to be to stymie all hope of an easy entrance or egress? You know the ones (particularly beloved, it seems, of double-glazing installers), where all manner of upward and downward movements are required before you can even think of unlocking or opening the damn thing. And then it takes it into its head to do a weird tilting thing: who on earth wants a TILTING door, for heaven's sake? Where, oh where, is Michael Caine's *Italian Job* safe-blower when you need him?!

Concrete

See That horrid concrete section of the M25

Constant changes to dietary advice

Carbs good, carbs bad. Meat good, meat bad. Veg good, veg bad. Fat…sugar…fruit…juice…butter…alcohol…coffee – in the past couple of decades there can hardly be a food/drink type that hasn't been successively praised as the holy grail of healthy eating, then comprehensively dissed months later as near-lethal in the next fatuous bit of dodgy research that does the rounds. I know it's utterly tedious, but isn't it mind-blowingly obvious that the originator of the phrase 'moderation in all things' had a point in regard to what we eat and drink? Well, apart from claret and gin, naturally (note the sly introduction of the wholesome overtone in that phrase), where I've yet to discover in what way either is anything but good for one's physical and mental state – though I do remember reading that the demise of Jennifer Paterson of *Two Fat Ladies* fame was hastened by a long-term overdose of quinine originating from an overindulgence in G and T. As a way of minimising THAT potential risk one could always resort to pink gin, I suppose, though no doubt some government-funded researcher will soon announce that Angostura bitters is a near-neighbour to arsenic on the lethal liquids scale.

See also Super-hydration

Content warnings

I do hope I'm not alone in thinking, when a warning comes up before a TV transmission, that we can expect 'nudity, sex, swearing etc', Oh goody! But what is WRONG with people studying Eng. Lit. that they have to be warned that there's a bit of nastiness in *King Lear*, or a bit of sex malarkey in *Lady Chatterley's Lover*, for instance, or frightening stuff in (unbelievably) *Harry Potter and the Philosopher's Stone*? Putting aside the weirdness of English students studying *Harry Potter* at University – dear God, those are the bits we used to most look forward to, as relief from the interminable worthiness of, say, *Middlemarch*. The time will come when even *Just William* books will have to come in a plain cover and with a content warning about the sexist treatment of Violet Elizabeth Bott or the aggression displayed by The Outlaws, in the same way as the dated – some might say, slightly iffy – views of Enid Blyton may have to be given 'context'. Yep, we ARE all going to hell in a handcart.

See also No platforming, Cancel culture

Corkscrews

See Useless corkscrews

Crazy paving

It's not exactly Gaudí, is it? Or indeed crazy. Just slightly mental. Especially when it's broken-up concrete and not even stone. Whoever the first 'crazy' was, he should have been locked up in Bedlam and the key broken up and imbedded in a small strip of cement as a warning to others. Dig the stuff up and substitute some smart gravel or a strip of neat tarmac. Thank you.

Creamer

What exactly IS that stuff you find on those cluttered tea trays in the rooms of the worst sort of hotels? Granted, it's cream-coloured, but that's about as far as it goes. It's not cream. It's not milk. It looks for all the world like one of the contents of one of those tiny 'matchpots' of paint you can buy to test a colour before you launch into painting a whole room. With a similarly slightly pungent, off-putting aroma. Creamer has a quality about it that renders tea with it added particularly horrid but is equally almost undrinkable in instant coffee. Avoid at all costs, naturally (unlike the product. Hoho).

Cruise liners

Wherever you are in the world, you just KNOW when a cruise liner has docked. Dubrovnik…Bordeaux…Quebec…Barcelona…Cannes. Suddenly, a relatively civilised place – albeit often already enduring a surfeit of trippers – becomes pretty much unbearable, as hordes of unfit, pasty-faced cruise ship passengers disembark to terrorise the town. Even half a mile from the docks, the likely limit of their perambulations, you can identify them from their uniform and the way they ask things like, 'Tell me, what country are we in?'

And when they're at sea, for all the world, cruise liners resemble nothing so much as an ungainly block of flats, almost certainly awash with all manner of ghastly tummy bugs (and hey, I wrote this BEFORE Covid-19!), no doubt first acquired at 'the captain's table'. And there are SO MANY OF THEM. No wonder places like Santorini are beginning to ration their arrival, if not ban them from visiting altogether. I read somewhere that some elderly widows have been known to sell up entirely on land and spend their sunset years traversing the globe on a boat called something like *Twilight Nightmare of the Seas*. What a grim prospect. If, like me (and I suspect all yachtsmen), you're more than a little allergic to them, you might gain a few moments' amusement by looking online for videos titled things like 'cruise liners in distress'. Schadenfreude isn't normally a nice reaction but sometimes it's just impossible not to enjoy.

See also The wrong (kind of) trousers, Bumbags (Vol. I)

Cultural appropriation

Time was when having a tequila party and getting everyone to wear a sombrero was innocent fun. It obviously still is, but we're not allowed to think like that. For many years there was a Mexican restaurant in Notting Hill Gate where dinners were enlivened by the compulsory wearing of a well-abused sombrero. In this new Dark Age, the chances are that even a swig of tequila gets you plonked on the naughty step, let alone demeaning the denizens of somewhere like Coatzacoalcos by affecting their style of headgear.

And talking of Notting Hill, not long ago Adele got a bashing in right-on media for her Bantu-style hair twists, combined with a Jamaican bikini to celebrate Carnival (I believe the 'the' is redundant in this context, just in case you think I'm becoming slipshod) in…wait for it…Notting Hill…from where she hails. Yet the same day *The Times* ran an ad for online shopping featuring a girl of colour with dramatic, straightened gingery hair – presumably culturally appropriating 'Celticnicity'. Can someone PLEASE set out the rules here? I need to know if the 'vicars and tarts' dress code is still acceptable in impolite society, or 'French onion-sellers', or 'Star Wars' costumes.

Culture

See Popular culture

Cummerbunds

A strange garment strangely de rigueur amongst DJ-wearing chaps during the Swinging Sixties. Typically made of silk or velvet or – worse – some man-made fabric such as crimplene, this was thought by many to disguise the onset of the beer belly, but in fact only served to accentuate it. As an evening wore on, this contraption tended to collapse in on itself, narrowing from perhaps a foot in 'depth' to an inch or two, and forming an impenetrable barrier when it came to 'pointing percy at the porcelain' or attempting to disrobe with the intention of performing a service to a young lady. Best consigned to the dressing-up box or generously donated to the likes of Oxfam, where it will languish for several years before finally finding its rightful home with thousands of others – some of dubious virulent shades of colour – in a landfill officially designated for the purpose.

See also Fake bow ties

Cussedness/contrariness for the sake of it

Behaviour taught in the advanced stages of training to be a traffic warden/border control 'officer', police 'person', librarian – or indeed any junior 'customer-facing' role that involves petty officialdom. A couple of examples will suffice to illustrate the syndrome. Some years ago I decided to 'road test' this theory with one of my daughters as we made to exit Passport Control at Bordeaux airport (assiduous readers will recall that decades of experience at the decidedly uncuddly Mérignac airport have given me mountains of material for commentary such as this). 'When you go through, offer your boarding card as well as your passport,' I said. Obediently – unusually, I grant you – she obeyed. Then, lo and behold, our man in the kiosk thrust back her boarding card. 'Pas necessaire,' he grunted. You know what's coming, don't you? Next in line, I offered just my passport. 'Boarding card?' he demanded.

Now, it's just conceivable that official policy had changed in the nanoseconds between our two exchanges, but you'd have to admit that it's unlikely: I leave it to you to judge whether – perhaps – he was, like so many in his position, merely being awkward for the sake of it.

As item number two for the prosecution, I give you a relatively recent experience on the M3 – dating in fact from the era when paper tax discs on cars were replaced by an 'online' 'service'. One morning, like pretty much everyone else in the fast lane, I was proceeding in an orderly fashion at approx. 84 mph when a high-powered police car flashing a multitude of blue and white lights swept past as I moved into the middle lane, before swerving in front of me and braking dramatically. I moved into the inside lane, at which point the police car switched lanes violently in front of me again and one of the 'officers' started gesticulating dramatically that I should go into Fleet Services. Now this is a pretty vile place at the best of times, as you may well be aware, but it was about to become rather more horrid than usual. The police BMW swerved in front of me, *Sweeney* style, obviously in case I was about to start a dramatic chase. At this point I should perhaps mention that I was driving a fairly ordinary, pretty much new Mercedes in fairly reasonable nick without those spinning hubcaps beloved of 'dealers' and wasn't wearing bling jewellery, wrap-around sunglasses and four-thousand-pound trainers.

I got out of the car, as I believe you're best advised to do, fully expecting these 'servants of the public' to shout out 'ADOPT THE POSITION!!' But no, I was just confronted with the usual, macho arrogance on uttering the dreaded phrase, 'What seems to be the trouble, officer?' as one of the two prowled round the car, I assume looking for – well, I can't imagine what. The usual questions – 'Do you know how fast you were going?', 'Where's your licence?', 'Do you come here often?' – were followed by, 'And where are you going?' 'Geneva', I replied. Having next had to provide details of just why I might be going to such an outlandish destination, the more aggressive of the two said, 'Well, you might well not be going ANYWHERE.' This dramatic overkill and the suspense before they revealed my appalling misdemeanour was eventually resolved. In a nutshell, because of some bureaucratic oversight the reminder that I should renew the tax disc had never arrived, and I had no idea that it was a full TWO MONTHS out of date – and hey, it was – what – a couple of hundred quid.

Now you try telling me that I was the only driver in that predicament during the change-over from offline to online, and moreover that this was the only pair of cops gleefully doing something similar to unwitting ne'er-do-wells like yours truly during that period. M'lud, I rest my case.

Cut flowers

What do they DO to flowers you purchase from the florist that means there's no fragrance?! It's like buying a bottle of claret and discovering that the alcohol content is a measly 1% rather than a healthy 12 or 13.

And while I'm on about cut flowers – why do tulips flop? I know all about changing the water, trimming off the leaves, and even the old wives' tale of dropping a copper coin in the vase. But still they look as though a decent dose of Viagra is the only solution likely to work, but twenty minutes uprightness (allegedly) once a day is surely not ideal for any self-respecting flower arrangement…

See also Alcohol content of wine

Cycle helmets

If you're storming down the gravelly hairpins down the back of the Col d'Aubisque in a fine drizzle at something like 60 mph with maybe a hundred of the world's best cyclists breathing down your neck, then I completely get the need for a cycle helmet. But if you're pootling along a country lane in Somerset or you're a child on a bike with stabilisers pottering round the local park – is it REALLY necessary? You should try going down Marlow Hill (one in ten, since you ask) in High Wycombe decades before the cycling helmet first saw the light of day, on a battered racing bike and being dared not to touch your brakes until you're almost at the bottom: I can assure you that the best bit was the wind in your hair, not the comforting feel of reinforced plastic keeping it in place. Oh, and surviving intact. Funny that.

And the jury is still very definitely out on their efficacy in general – as in, do they encourage a misplaced sense of invulnerability in the cyclist and an undue lack of concern on the part of passing motorists? I know where I stand. Oh, and they're so not flattering. A bit like Lycra on the wrong-shaped body, but let's not go there. Then, of course, there's the issue of 'helmet hair', which means that, try as you might to shake your locks loose when the helmet comes off, they will resolutely stay in that flattened, matted shape for the rest of the day.

Cyclists

See Selfish – or should I say, lethal bastard – cyclists

D

Defence procurement

From those wonderful MoD people (see Vol. I) that brought you aircraft carriers that leaked and had no planes, and destroyers that couldn't cope with warmish seas and move and shoot at the same time, I offer you tanks that have cost billions but can't go over 20 mph without turning their occupants to jelly and – you can see this coming a mile off – are incapable of firing their gun on the move. I rather think that particular trick was even mastered in the mud of Flanders over a century ago…

Designer handbags

Look, girls – or any deluded chaps out there for some bizarre reason temporarily self-identifying as girls – LET'S GET REAL. A handbag is merely a smallish container, held by a carrying strap of some appropriate length, in which you can handily keep a few useful items, viz. lipstick, emergency contraceptives, ibuprofen, mascara, a small quantity of cash, a credit card, a pack of tissues, hipflask etc. At a pinch, maybe also a mobile phone, business card or small diary, or your passport in case you're feeling exotic or spontaneous or merely harbouring an unfulfilled sense of adventure. IT DOESN'T NEED TO COST TEN THOUSAND POUNDS OR BE TRYING TO MAKE SOME KIND OF STATEMENT.

A sensible handbag could come from your local market or charity shop, and should cost at most a fiver. Some people find a plastic carrier bag perfectly serviceable (in fact, I even read recently that some ludicrous over-hyped brand has 'reinvented' the plastic carrier bag as a handbag. And is selling it for HUNDREDS OF POUNDS).

And seriously, you don't need one of every colour in the rainbow just to 'match your outfit'. One simple handbag in a suitably neutral colour such as black (though not beige, obviously) should suffice, unless your self-image is so worthless that you need perhaps a second as a 'prop'. And please, don't manhandle (the clue's in the name, dear) a handbag the size of an elephant's scrotum: something roughly with the dimensions of an A4 envelope should serve most needs.

Dijon mustard

Make no mistake. This dastardly French invention has no place on our tables or in our kitchens. Mustard should be mustard yellow (see?!), hot – and English. Preferably from Colman's of Norwich and made fresh for the occasion by carefully mixing the DSF (double superfine, for those yearning to add to their general knowledge, on account of one of the earliest trademarked processes by which a combination of sieves with different-sized holes produced a better-quality powder: this book aims to educate as well as divert) powder with the appropriate quantity of fresh tap water…

A grey-yellow (the name of a leading brand, Grey Poupon, is a bit of a giveaway – not as bright as they thought, the French, eh?!), slightly slimy substance, Dijon mustard has a winey quality about it and reeks of vinegar. No matter that they claim it contains wine: the place for that is in a wine glass or a good old-fashioned British dish like coq au vin. Expressly NOT in mustard; most of us are not so desperate that the mere suggestion of wine in a product will propel us to wolf it down. Oh, on reflection…

Disappearing hairbrushes

What IS IT that makes my hairbrush so appealing that it's always being commandeered by others? Even when I've been given one for my personal use by Father Christmas, it will have disappeared to the other side of the bedroom by the end of January, buried under a small mountain of nail varnish bottles. And then – gone for ever. Tell me I'm not paranoid. And please – tell me I'm not alone.

Doorhandles

See Complicated doorhandles

Dramatic gum-chewing

Nothing much wrong with a small quantity of chewing gum – under the right circumstances and in the right place, which is obviously NOT on the pavement. But what IS wrong is gum-chewing *exhibitionism*. Honestly, no one else wants to know you're at it: they don't want to see dramatic facial movements, or hear loud smacking/chewing noises, and they certainly don't want to SEE evidence of it. So please – enjoy chewing gum discreetly and with the minimum of visible activity – and don't get me started on what happens when you're 'done chewing'. A simple comparison between the streets of Singapore and London should suffice…

Dramatic public sneezing

Look, it's not a command performance: if you HAVE to sneeze, kindly turn away from everyone else and cup your hands over your face as you erupt. Even better, cover your head in advance with an outsize jiffy bag, or handkerchief if no jiffy bag is to hand. Whatever – don't show off and look around, supremely pleased with yourself, after the event. It might have been big…but it's not clever (unlike this author, who first penned these words before coronavirus struck).

See also Absurdly dramatic public yawning

Drivers, crap

See Bloody car drivers who sneak up on your inside before pulling into the sensible gap you'd left behind the car in front

Dummies

I know a daughter-in-law who's going to have a major lapse of humour about this, but out of a sheer sense of civic duty I must call into question the need, role, purpose, point etc of the ghastly 'comforter' or 'pacifier', as I believe it is known in some circles. To my mind, seeing a child impaled on a piece of germ-infested rubber in a shape that calls to mind an over-developed Page 3 girl on a very cold day is a bit like watching the suffering of a cat forced to wear a collar with a bell on it. Sooo not good. Am I alone in finding Maggie's incessant dummy-sucking one of the few elements in *The Simpsons* that jars? I mean, what's wrong with a thumb, the way nature intended, for goodness' sake?!

There must be better ways to wean her off the dummy?

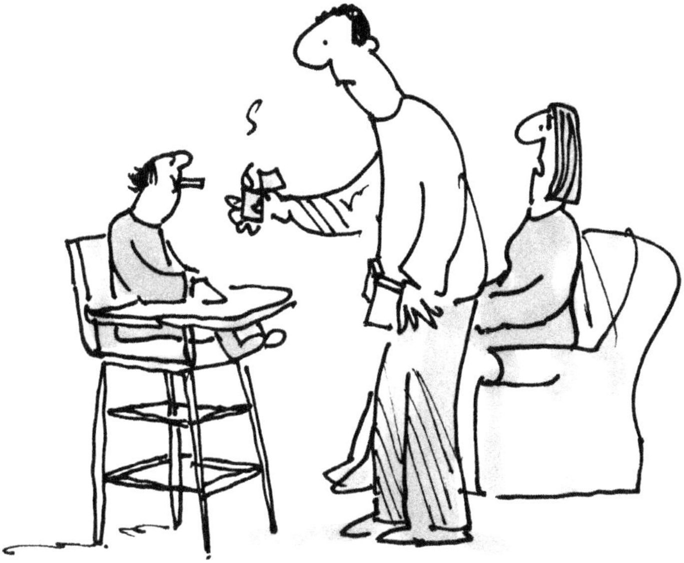

E

Eating in theatres, cinemas and similarly inappropriate venues

What is it about cinemas, theatres and so on that induces in so many people a hunger so urgent that it has to be satisfied immediately? And why can it only be sated by food that is beyond smelly – and noisy? I mean…popcorn…crisps…pizza…a Big Mac?!?!? Back in the day a small tub of artificial ice cream or a little plastic beaker of Kia-Ora would suffice, but one cinema near us I try to avoid allows people to eat a serious dinner a few rows away from where I'm trying to get forty winks. Wine, I get. Whisky, sure. Maybe even that dismal alternative, a 'soft drink'. But a mound of tacos on a sharing platter covered in the most pungent of heated cheese – oh puhlease.

Eco-friendly firelighters

You don't have to be a strict adherent to the notion of nominative determinism to expect a product described as a firelighter to be able to light a fire. But the ones described as eco-friendly are about as much use as moth-killer with a twentieth of the potency of good old mothballs or New Age feeble weedkillers that seem to encourage the spread of knee-high thistles in your gravel drive. Steer clear of the ones that look like a thin block of fudge, neatly pre-sliced, or the ones that for all the world look like the yummy hairy kataifi you might enjoy with a drop of Filfar liqueur after a Greek meal. They do not do what it says on the tin. Whoever coined the phrase 'about as much use as a chocolate teapot' was clearly genius – but they clearly hadn't encountered the eco-friendly firelighter.

Eco setting

See The 'eco' setting on washing machines and dishwashers

Eggs

See Nausea-inducing fried eggs

Egregious

Why is everything suddenly egregious?

See also Cohort

Electric lawnmowers

For all of those weary of that wretched pull-cord that as like as not fails to start the engine on a petrol-driven mower, the electric alternative might seem a good idea. No more smart-arsed neighbours informing you that you've flooded the engine and need to bake the spark plug at 200 degrees for 15 minutes before there's any chance it will start – by which time it will almost certainly have started raining.

So you consign the 'old-tech' mower to the back of the shed and embark on your journey with the gleaming new electric version. In all likelihood your first outing will be fairly satisfactory, but this is only lulling you into a false sense of security. The next time out, you are almost certain to slice straight through the electric cable in a fit of absent-mindedness ('What's THAT doing there… oh…b★gger!'). If you don't kill yourself in the process, you will

Oh can I call you back? My husband's cut through the electric cable again

then have to endure years of continually reconnecting the bits of torn wire together, which will always be a weak point and come apart at the slightest tug when it gets stuck in the rockery. Whoever said grass-cutting could be therapeutic?

Espadrilles

Always just too small or just too big.

If I buy a pair of 43s, they'll never go on easily, even if they've been 'broken in', so I'll end up slopping around with the Quarter, as I believe it's called, crushed under my heel, for all the world as if I were wearing a pair of mules – and how wrong is that? The alternative is to use the flat end of a large spoon or your index finger (in which case, that nasty paper cut you suffered will reopen for the hundredth time) to persuade the shoe to 'accept' your foot, and jam it in there forcefully.

If on the other hand I buy a pair of 44s, I already know what will happen. They'll go on easily. Too easily. Which means that after they've worn in they'll forever be too loose, and I'll end up wearing them in the style of mules (see above). Not a good look.

And while I'm banging on about espadrilles – ideally French-made not thrown together in some godforsaken far-flung corner of the world, in which case there's at a least a small chance they'll last a fortnight's holiday – can anyone explain to me why, when you've dropped them to the ground after walking up the beach barefoot, they NEVER land the right way up, in the right formation, so giving one the possibility of easing them on gently whilst simultaneously manhandling half a hundredweight of seaside entertainment malarkey?

See also Paper cuts

Exposed bum cracks

On a beach…by the pool…in a 'gentlemen's club' (oh, the irony!)…a hint of bum crack above a slightly misplaced knicker or bikini bottom can be – well, rather pleasing under the right circs. But otherwise, in both male and female contexts – and especially male – this is obviously to be deplored. I can't be the only person to shudder and quickly avert my gaze when several inches of bottom cleavage are wantonly exposed, by a total stranger, in uncomfortably close proximity. Particularly when – there's no very neat way of saying this – it looks somewhat 'untended'. Have these accidental (I hope) exhibitionists not been introduced to that highly practical contraption, the belt? It's been around at least since the Bronze Age, so you would have thought that even the most antediluvian amongst us might have cottoned on to the principle by now.

Then, of course, there's the issue of 'thongs' (and I don't mean what Australians weirdly mean by flip-flops). The maximum exposure of a shapely buttock or two is rightly to be applauded, but does ANYBODY get on with a thong? I can't help thinking that they achieve the opposite of what's intended as they disappear, semi-permanently, into the very nether regions that their role is to obscure.

F

Facebook

No, this isn't the usual – but perfectly understandable – whinge about how ghastly 97 per cent of the postings on this wretched 'service' are, though naturally I'd be happy to oblige. This is more about the ghastliness of the organisation itself. It is, of course, even more than that otherwise once-proud monolith British Airways, breath-taking in its arrogance and remoteness from real people. Have you ever tried to contact it with a real concern? Hmm.

Not long ago I launched a brand with a series of different designs designed to cause a small amount of merriment. One featured a rendition of Michelangelo's *David* on one side, with Botticelli's *Venus* on the reverse. The joke was, you could switch heads – rather like in those children's flip books where the man ends up wearing the bikini etc etc. So Venus ended up with – to put it politely – a todger. A stone one, obviously. No offence given, and no offence suffered (unless Mary Whitehouse has come back from hiding behind the sofa in the firmament to haunt us). These are two of the most reproduced images in all of human history: there can't be many who haven't already glimpsed the not-so-private parts of these two works of art. But because Facebook's hideous sinister computers decided they were deeply and dangerously pornographic, my ad campaign was pulled without redress and I had to remove them from the website and withdraw them for sale before this 'force for good' would agree to me recommencing marketing. This took three months and destroyed our launch.

It gets better. Once we were back in their good books, within days of starting to spend serious money with them, all hell broke loose. A bunch of apparently Vietnamese fraudsters had somehow got the better of their much-vaunted oh-so-secure systems, had latched onto our campaign and were systematically draining our bank account. It took over a month for that one to get sorted out, during which time we were perforce 'off air' again. And you guessed it – no one of any significance was contactable throughout this entire episode. Meantime, inexplicably, the organisation goes from strength to strength, unlike our inoffensive, well-intentioned little brand which has yet to recover from the battering it received.

Meta my arse.

Fake bald heads

What IS it with young men nowadays?! You'll be bald soon enough, so why go and shave off all your crowning glory ahead of time? Especially if, as so often seems to be the case, your unnaturally bald head has all the aesthetic appeal of a mishappen, much-scarred outcrop of granite only lately trimmed of its protective layer of lichen by a blast of air straight from the Urals.

And then, to compound the effect, as often as not the owner of the unnecessarily bald head will have a burgeoning beard a few inches below it. You can't help feeling that if the whole thing – the head, I mean – were upside down, the appearance would be somewhat more as God intended. I reckon this phase started in the eighties – no idea why, something to do with the thuggish look perpetrated by *EastEnders* maybe? But why would anyone other than a wannabe bouncer think that imitating a thug could be a desirable ambition? In 1970s adland, you couldn't work on the Gillette account if you had facial hair (unless you were a lady…JOKING), but there cannot be many careers these days where artificial baldness is a prerequisite.

Fake bows on Christmas wrapping

These invariably come with a little self-adhesive sticker on the bottom, presumably with the aim of making life that little bit easier in the supposedly high-pressure period in the run-up to Christmas (why IS it so often described in these terms, I wonder? ANOTHER First World problem). But in fact the result is the opposite of what their manufacturers presumably intend (unless they're like the chief villain in some Bond-style caper, bit by tiny bit intending to destroy the morale of mankind and so achieve world domination). Don't tell me you've ever been able nimbly to peel off the backing tape, despite the fact that it's theoretically split into two halves with little arrows purporting to help you in this endeavour. I always end up wielding the sharpest pair of scissors available to separate the sticky bit from the rest and end up sporting Elastoplast on two fingers – and then chucking the damn thing in the bin. As for the Elastoplast-covered fingers, as a former church organist I can tell you that really DOES make for a high-pressure period in the run-up to Christmas…

See Elastoplast (Vol. I)

Fake bowties

There is obviously only one faux pas more pathetic than wearing a bowtie that's pre-tied (whether clip-on or fastened to a neck band) and that's having the gall to half remove it halfway through an evening to leave the pre-tied bow dangling from your collar for all the world like a sinister pipistrelle dangling from a limestone cliff. SO not a good look: aside from it being self-evidently unattractive as a 'look', it is never clever to draw attention to one's own sartorial solecisms. Other people's, of course, are absolutely fair game.

Familiarity

See Inappropriate familiarity

Far more different kinds of lightbulbs than can really be necessary

I've already (in Vol. I) banged on about the absurdity and inefficacy of low-energy lightbulbs, but there's a side-effect which I was remiss in not discussing. That is to say, where there once was a ludicrous multiplicity of lightbulb formats, this has now perforce doubled. What was wrong with the good old 60- or 100-watt normal bayonet fitting? I ask. That was all one required in a more innocent age. Now there are screw-ins of varying dimensions as well as bayonets, fatboy versions and thin little chaps, not to mention all those different versions of mini-spotlights, LEDs, strip lights and the like. Then, of course, you also have those tiny bulbs in the fridge or the extractor hood. And sod's law, of course, when it comes to replacing a dud one (and please don't give me the canard that these new long-life types last any longer than the tried-and-tested 'proper' lightbulbs), you can be sure that, however much you rifle through your box of spares, the one you actually need is never there.

Fatuous pronouncements over public address systems

I thought I'd nailed this problem comprehensively in Volume I, but it seems that EasyJet weren't paying attention. The contract with the 'poor man's William Hague' has clearly been renewed, and among other useless phrases deployed in an inappropriately matey soft

Yorkshire accent he now enjoins passengers to 'have a greeeaaat flight'. Do the management have NO sense of irony? Surely it's obvious that there's more chance of a great flight – even surrounded by all that orange – if he'd only shut up. It reminds me of that ghastly fanfare that Ryanair used to deploy every single time one of their flights arrived on time. Aaaaaaarrrgggghhhh!! I much preferred the old habit whereby elderly Italian matrons would loudly applaud if an Alitalia plane managed to land at all. At least that was spontaneous.

Fatuous questions

Aside from the vile 'Everything all right with your meal?' query from a waitress, don't you hate almost more than anything being asked by someone in a service industry, 'You all right there?' or, 'You OK?' What's wrong with an old-fashioned, 'May I help you?' It's frankly none of your business whether I feel OK or not – all I want is for you to take my order and fulfil it with as little flannel as possible. Thank you.

See also 'Can I get…?'

Feet on seats

Just because feet rhymes with seat is no justification for placing them in close proximity. Don't you hate it when a yobbo lounges with his grubby shoes on the train seat that in all probability your derriere will be resting on the next day. And yet, and yet… how many of us dare risk intervening, in fear of what kind of retribution might follow? A sensible halfway house might be to proffer your folded newspaper as a kind of modern-day foot-related antimacassar, but even that might be viewed as a form of sarcasm. Which, of course, it is. And in another phrase which is sooo à la mode, a wonderful instance of 'passive-aggressive behaviour' which will almost inevitably end in tears. Yours, obvs.

Fellow guests on the lookout for someone more interesting

Is there ANYTHING more irritating than being in conversation with someone and becoming painfully aware that you're of less interest than someone else who just hove into sight? Believe it or not, this HAS happened to me. It's like chatting with someone who's got crossed eyes: you're never sure whether it's their disability or lack of engagement that gives the impression they're looking anywhere but you. It gives rise to a strong temptation to say, 'But you're boring me', whereas in true English traditions of politesse you're more likely to say something like, 'But I must let you go' or, 'Sorry, I'm monopolising you.' This syndrome is particularly pronounced at conferences, where having covertly (and yet, obviously, obvs) ascertained your name and title from the little badge hanging round your neck, the person you're talking to spends the whole time looking over your shoulder, in the hope that someone more important/interesting/attractive/likely to buy them a drink has just arrived. Dontchajusthatethem?

See also Apologising for no reason

Film credits

I well remember staying in my seat for easily ten minutes after the end of the excellent Sam Mendes' film *1917* just to take in the extraordinary credits, the longest I think I have seen and almost as impressive as the movie itself. But I really dislike it when, on the smaller screen, these are compressed or speeded up or both, so you never catch the name of the performer who played the part of X or who composed the music or – I should disclose a personal interest here (no, not ME, that would be silly) – the make-up artist? Credit where credit is due, say I.

Fingernails

What IS it with those miniscule prickly bits that appear from time to time either side of your fingernails that are almost invisible but phenomenally irritating? They resist all efforts to excise them, whether by teeth, nail scissors or other means, and get more and more sore in the way that only really tiny blemishes have a habit of doing. Then, suddenly one day, just as they appeared from nowhere, they're gone. Why bother to appear in the first place is what I want to know.

And do please tell me, has an international agreement been signed to govern the appearance of the fingernails of porn stars? They all seem to be overlong and squared off in a particularly unattractive way, a bit like the end of the blade of an old-fashioned butterknife. And the last half an inch or so is invariably flat white in colour, so drawing attention to its seriously poor taste. Could porn film casting directors please take note and offer up a palette of pleasing nail colours and nail-shape templates, so that viewers could enjoy a little more variety in this aspect of their entertainment, if in no other aspect such as storylines, dialogue, positions, lingerie etc etc?   And please – PLEASE – don't enquire how I came about this arcane piece of knowledge (by accident, honestly guv, when I'd keyed in 'lovable puppies'…).

Finishing times of live performances

How can one be expected to book an 'after-show dinner' with only the foggiest notion (sometime before midnight) of when the performance is going to end? Shouldn't it be a basic bit of information included on a booking form? For example, there's a huge difference in the length of time that Bach's *Mass in B Minor* takes to sing if you include all the repeats as originally stipulated. The same probably goes for a 'popular music' concert, what with all the screaming and caterwauling typically involved.

Flatpack furniture

Aeons ago there was a massive furnishing company called MFI who one suspects had as its mission statement (dread phrase) 'inducing hair-tearing-out despair in the well-intentioned, striving but not-so-well-heeled middle classes'. They were in the vanguard of the flatpack furniture revolution, whereby a family could buy a whole houseful of furnishings for little more than the price of a round of drinks. The only problem was that a key item was invariably missing from the box – some screws of a particular dimension, say, an Allen key, or even one of two wardrobe doors. Just as bad, like as not you'd find that the holes for a fastening joining two bits of wood together were misaligned, so that the bedside cabinet was wonky for evermore and was likely to collapse if you so much as sneezed in the same room.

All that notwithstanding, the habit of buying household goods disassembled – a bit like the fad for deconstructed puddings, which saw restaurants serving, for instance, the constituent parts of an

It's my flatpack wardrobe which is now my flat pack barbecue!!

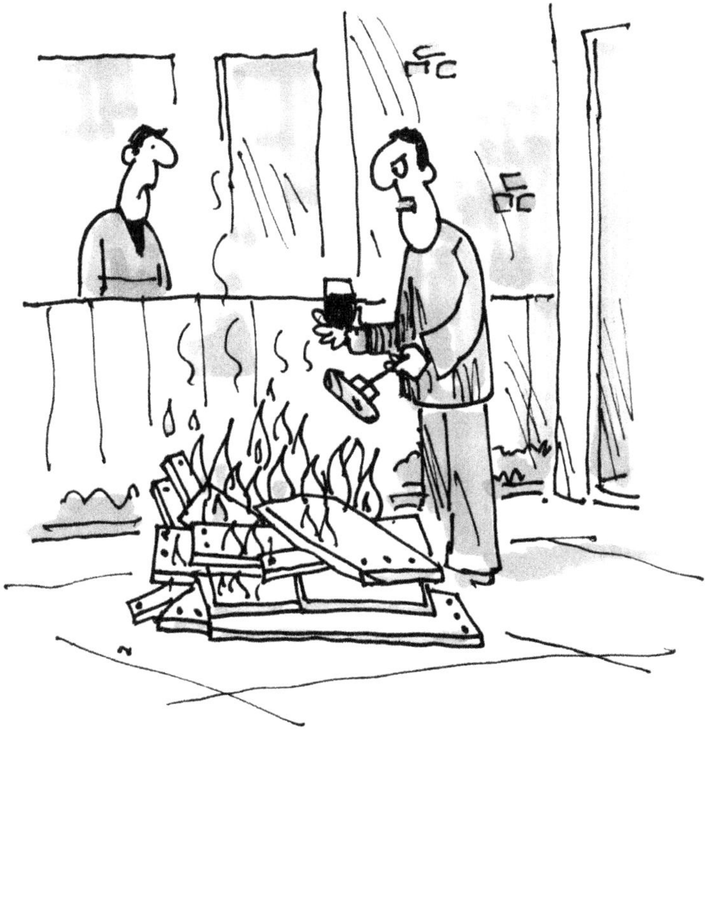

apple crumble in small heaps on a plate – has become ingrained. What this means, for example, is that it is near-impossible to buy things like a barbecue without having to invest a day of your time in its manufacture and a small fortune on a toolkit. And I guarantee that the 'misaligned holes syndrome' lives on – and you try bodging this in metal plates rather than bits of soft, chunky pine. Hah! Your barbecue will now match your bedside cabinet, but not in the way you imagined.

Flowers

See Cut flowers

Foodservice manuals

'Everything all right with your meee-al?' Dread words, issued to you in a certain type of eatery, within moments of you taking your first bite of food. If that kind of question is being asked, the answer, almost inevitably, will be, 'No'. But of course you can't speak with your mouth full, so you invariably nod bleakly and hope the interrogation ends as quickly as it started.

Chances are this questioning will have been preceded by such gems – in a sing-song voice, much-rehearsed – as 'Still or sparkling warteh?' or 'Ice 'n' a slice with that?!' Admit it, you should have left there and then, but going against the strong hints from your inner self, you gave the place one more chance. Wrong choice: you have encountered the sub-world of the foodservice manual and its manufactured foibles. This will likely consist of a large ring-binder containing laminated pages which bear such examples as I've given and a lot of poor-quality photographs of what a finished dish should look like. I say SHOULD look like, but that, of course, is irony. You can't tell me that suitably attired 'nippies', back in the days of good old Joe Lyons, ever needed a manual to show them how to give a customer a good time…

French bureaucracy

I know this has been the subject of innumerable diatribes over the years, but unless you've actually experienced it (and trust me, over almost forty years, I HAVE, in spades…if I'm still allowed to say that), you come to realise that the inspiration behind Kafka's writing wasn't his employment in a Prague-based insurance company, but rather an attempt to install a telephone line in rural France.

I've also come to the conclusion that Joseph Heller didn't come up with the idea of *Catch 22* when he was in the US forces in World War II but instead while trying to upgrade the electricity supply to his *maison secondaire*.

Everything you hear about French bureaucracy is true: the telecommunications company that will only accept instructions by snail mail; the form in septuplicate that you have to complete to begin the process of installing a swimming pool; the requirement to scrawl '*lu et approuve*' on every single page of a document, however inconsequential; the near-impossibility of *rematriculating* a foreign-registered car – even if it is a Citroen…

To be fair, ghastly bureaucracy is, of course, a universal scourge. I had a classic 'online experience' not long ago – in English. The mobile app of my UK bank (the one that was foisted on the UK taxpayer in 2008) decided for no discernible reason that 'my face didn't fit' any longer, in that it was no longer recognised by the biometric thingummy as…my face. Which hadn't changed THAT much in the few days since it last scanned it. A long wait for a call centre to respond resulted in my being advised that the mobile app would no longer work until it was fixed at their end – my face wasn't the problem, the app was, which was a relief of sorts…but no problem, I would be able to use my laptop to access what was left of MY money. So off I scurried to my desk, to make some inconsequential but necessary transactions. You can probably guess what happened next: before any of my instructions could be carried out on my laptop, my identity had to be verified in the mobile app on my phone… which demanded that I revealed my face. Which it didn't like (in fairness, quite a few don't). And so, back to the call centre I went, which unsurprisingly was unsurprised. Had I thought of visiting a branch, they enquired? When I replied that I was frightened of showing my face there, they failed to see the joke, which probably explains why they were employed by a call centre and not as a gag-writer on 'I'm Sorry, I Haven't a Clue'.

French lavatories

There must be millions of nostalgic holidaymakers who yearn for the 'two footprints' style of French bog, with all that it embodied years ago as an emblem of the start of the summer hols. In their place have come all manner of peculiar contrivances, manufactured from all sorts of materials, in a startling variety of designs, given that they only have one function, i.e. to help one discharge effluent of whatever type in as easy and decent a fashion as possible. But perhaps the oddest aspect is something to which no one has been able to provide a satisfactory answer – and believe me, I've asked. Why is it that the French have a habit of constructing a vast cubicle and then putting the sole lavatory in it in the farthest reaches, crammed so tightly against a corner that even the most modest of 'manspreaders' has to sit side saddle. Is there a movement across the Channel (lavatorial mild pun intended) of which I'm unaware that permits the ingress of a sizeable audience to observe the performer at stool? Are you now half-expected to provide scatological entertainment, or is it merely an in-joke of the typically unfunny type that pervades the French airwaves in the early-evening schedules, and of which all Englishmen are in blissful ignorance?

They should instead take a leaf from the late-lamented Kim Tickell at the Tickell Arms in Cambridgeshire and connect the johnny machine to a loud bell in the bar, so that the user's embarrassment could be optimised and enjoyed by all as he exited. Much more inventive – like all British humour. Has there EVER been a funny French joke? I give you Marcel Marceau as evidence: has anyone normal ever laughed at his 'white-gloves-apparently-feeling-their-way-up a-window' act?

Full sex

Odd phrase sometimes deployed by tabloid newspapers to describe part of an encounter, typically as part of a 'kiss-and-tell' news item. Worryingly onomatopoeic, or is that just me? Does ANYONE normal ever use that phrase, as in a bloke showing off to his mates… 'D'you know what, I've just had FULL SEX with Tracey!!' And as for a 'a sex act', we've all known what THAT means since the well-publicised discovery of the Duchess of Argyll's supposedly scandalous polaroid. In the interest of calling a spade an effin' shovel, in the third decade of the twenty-first century can't we just refer to a BJ as a BJ, for pity's sake?

G

Garden centres

Retail outlets that pretty much put old-school nurseries out of business by selling all manner of plants, shrubs, trees and associated gardening paraphernalia in an environment that the modern amateur gardener found less 'challenging'. These then discovered that more money was to be made by 'delighting the customer'* through selling all manner of third-rate consumerist tat – especially pre-Christmas – and therefore dramatically reducing the space dedicated to horticultural activities, so that this is a now a token presence. So, you read it here first, Mr/Mrs/Ms Budding (geddit?) Entrepreneur: there is a looming market gap for a chain of outlets selling gardening perquisites and nothing else. You could even call them nurseries.

*For those not in the know, this has become the mantra of all wannabe star merchants. Forget prices, margins, quality etc etc – all you have to do is 'delight' your clientele. Now I don't know about you, but the only commercial context in which I have seen the word 'delight' appropriately used is in the brand name 'Fry's Turkish Delight'. All else is blatantly…well, b★★★★★★s.

Gin

See Self-important gins

Grazing

Acceptable behaviour in ruminants (e.g. cows, sheep). Thoroughly dismal behaviour in human beings. By all means have a few peanuts or crisps, eaten in a discreet fashion over the space of a few minutes, but do not turn this into a five-hour chompathon entailing all manner of snackfoods.

It's simple: a traditional 'fatboy' breakfast will set you up for the day; 'elevenses' accompanied by a biscuit if you must – never dunked – is allowable; luncheon is clearly necessary for most of us, most days (by which I do NOT mean a ragbag collection of foods consumed over a period of hours between 11 a.m. and 3.30 p.m. at your desk); afternoon tea is occasionally desirable (but NEVER, obviously, involving the use of a cake-stand); preprandial drinks may be taken of an evening, at which time a few small salty/savoury food items may briefly be consumed; followed by dinner/supper, depending on the circumstances and assuming that 'High Tea' has not been taken that day.

Any semi-continuous food consumption that joins these more formal occasions together, like ribbon development along an arterial road, is a shocking display of behaviour and just as unattractive.

See also Nibbles

Great sportsmen who are subsequently inappropriately hired as commentators

When I worked in the retail business a lifetime ago, it was customary for a hiring error to be repeated endlessly. A good shop manager would be promoted to be a regional manager, at which inevitably he/she failed. A good regional manager would be promoted to be, say, marketing director – at which he/she would invariably fail. In the same way, the qualities that made for an outstanding receptionist were unlikely to stand her (it was almost always a 'her') in good stead as the personal assistant to the chairman, notwithstanding her otherwise outstanding – ahem

ahem – talents. You wanted her to stay as a highly regarded, highly rewarded receptionist precisely because her qualities admirably suited the position (no sniggering at the back, please).

In the same way, it is the exception rather than the rule that a supreme sportsperson will make an outstanding commentator, never mind that their intimate knowledge of their sport is second to none. So, sadly, the brilliance that David Millar brings to his reporting of the Tour de France is not matched by the impenetrability of Sean Kelly on La Vuelta. Murray Walker of Formula One was a petrolhead not a driver, whereas for this writer Nigel Mansell was a driver *nonpareil* but utterly unsuited to the commentary box. I could drone on – cricket, soccer, rugby, you name it – but you get the drift.

Grim places of work

Look, I'm not talking about coalmines here, or a furniture showroom replaying the same ghastly soundtrack all day long, or even labouring as a cleaner on a cross-Channel ferry that's just docked after a choppy voyage in Storm Force 10. I am referring to those offices that used to be a hive of productive, computer – creative, even – industry but now consist entirely of serried ranks of dismal computer screens, staffed entirely by people wearing headphones whose idea of creative interaction is to send an email to their neighbour.

All those media companies that used to be abuzz with chatter (not all of it inappropriate, though that was obviously the best bit) are now only alive with the sub-buzz of computer noises and the click of keyboards. Nobody even moves, it seems, except for the excitement of a 'natural break' or to retrieve some morsel of food from the corporate fridge. Utterly soulless: it's very sad. Maybe WFH has at least in part been a reaction to the sheer tedium of so many places of work.

Gripper rods

If, like me, you've ever had to rip out some old carpet to attend to the floorboards underneath, then maybe you should skip to the next entry. Because you KNOW what it's going to be. Excruciating. However prewarned you are, however fastidious in your deployment of heavy-duty gloves, however high your pain threshold, how could handling a thin piece of wood with hundreds of unbelievably sharp pointy bits sticking out all along one side like the broken glass on a prison perimeter wall, and a host of nasty little nails sticking out the other, be anything other than – utterly excruciating? That's a gripper rod for you. The devil's handiwork. Best get a man in, so to speak.

Grotesque over-packaging of things purchased online

How many times do you receive a huge cardboard box, crammed with all manner of padding, stuffing etc, and eventually retrieve a small device that occupies at most 10 per cent of the capacity of the container? Apart from leading to crushing disappointment, you find yourself questioning all those newly established eco-friendly habits that as it happens bedevil your everyday life, only for all the brownie points you've worked so hard to accumulate to be erased from your 'account' by one enormous, unnecessary carbon footprint courtesy of Messrs Amazon et al.

Gum-chewing

See Dramatic gum-chewing

Oh great, this will be my new watch

H

Haggling, twenty-first-century style

I'm as much up for the kind of bargaining that cognoscenti employ in Istanbul's Grand Bazaar as anyone (hey, I once got the price of a fake-brand handbag down by 70 per cent!), but I really resent what goes on with so-called reputable companies who've enjoyed my custom for years – sometimes decades. And I'm not just talking about the business of 'churning' credit cards here, but the whole malarkey of proactively contacting a provider to query a bill and discovering that one is paying massively over the odds. Why should it be down to the customer to do this?!

My worst experience was with one of the country's best-known health insurance providers, whose annual fees had been climbing remorselessly annually, and with whom we'd been insured for something like thirty years. Patience having well and truly snapped, I embarked on a long and costly phone call. The upshot was that we were advised to cancel our antique policy and commence a fresh relationship as a newbie: at a stroke, our costs reduced by something like 60 per cent – several thousand pounds!

Emboldened by this, almost all my 'customer journeys' now follow a similar path, with comparable results – including with a well-known bank, Britain's best-known car support organisation, and the world's most famous charge card. All well and good in a way – but why should it be ME doing all the blagging and not the company, in the name of looking after their clientele? Attempts at inducing change from our ghastly governments have sadly not produced the same result.

Hairbrushes

See Disappearing hairbrushes

Hair products

Yes, occasionally one needs to wash one's hair. But several times daily, using an array of products that make your hair fuller/thinner/lusher/shinier/thicker/glossier/less dandruffy/easier to handle/curlier/straighter? And that can be for every conceivable hair type – dry, old, grey, brown, brunette, coloured, afro, black, blonde, young, long, short, you name it? Funny, isn't it, that the majority of the population is medium-length and mousy…and yet you never see a shampoo for that. Opportunity for a behemoth like P and G to tackle a whole sector, I'd have thought.

And then there's the whole fake science aspect too – what one brand for a while referred to coyly in its ads as 'here comes the science bit'. No, it's not science – it's fraud. All those reconstructed microscopic close-ups of supposedly helpful atoms doing their thing to individual hair follicles is just so much bunkum – probably lifted in their entirety from a GCSE biology textbook about eggs and sperm doing their thing in unpleasant close-up.

Half-term trips

These are short interludes – never short enough in the view of most sane people – in an already short enough school term, which among other things lead to London being impossible to navigate for work purposes. Their main reason for being is to enable tour operators, ferry companies, ski firms and the like to quintuple their prices, but this doesn't stop places like Luton Airport from becoming giant playgrounds overfull with caterwauling children for the best part of a fortnight. Their effect in France is to make the Alps un-skiable for anyone for weeks at a time because French schools are on a staggered system of half-terms which sees the slopes horrendously over-occupied for something like a month at the height of the season. Time was, when, for children of an earlier generation, half-term simply meant an extra half-hour in bed in the mornings. Not these days when little short of ten days in Acapulco will suffice for many. The solution? Simply abolish them and let school start half an hour later for a week in mid-term. Creative thinking, huh?

Harem pants

No doubt practicable wear in a harem, permitting as they do easy access and significant camouflage capabilities, but worn anywhere else they are obviously laughable. Look, love, the crotch of your trousers should at least be FAIRLY adjacent to your crotch – not two feet below it, swaying hither and thither in a somewhat unfanciable way. For pity's sake hitch 'em up..

Harrods

Not quite as irredeemably naff as when Mr Fayed owned it, with its gruesome memorial, but still – well, pretty naff. It is merely a fairly efficient machine for removing surplus monies from unwitting tourists, and as such you are best advised to walk on the north side of the Brompton Road, averting your eyes as you go.

Having to listen to other people's audible books

OK, it's not up there with the 'tsk tsk tsky tsss tsk' of the sound seeping from someone else's headphones, but the enforced eavesdropping occasioned by someone playing an audible book in your hearing – and I don't know why, but especially on their mobile – is, frankly, painful. It's not just that they're already halfway through whatever it is they're listening to, or indeed that the book is invariably very much NOT to your taste – it's the half-hearing someone you don't know, bleating away about something you don't care about, with a sound quality that's as like as not akin to the Home Service on a bad day in 1958. If this tome ever makes it to Audible, please accept my sincerest apologies in advance.

Having to show your boarding card at airport shops

Please somebody, tell me – WHAT'S all this about? Setting aside the fact that 'duty-free' is an all-but-meaningless term in the first place, why, if you choose to buy, for example, a copy of *The Times*, should you have to produce proof that you're about to board a plane? For God's sake, you're 'airside' already, what more do they need to know?!?

Home decorating

See The perils of painting

Houseflies

Why?

Sorry pal, this is a no fly zone!!

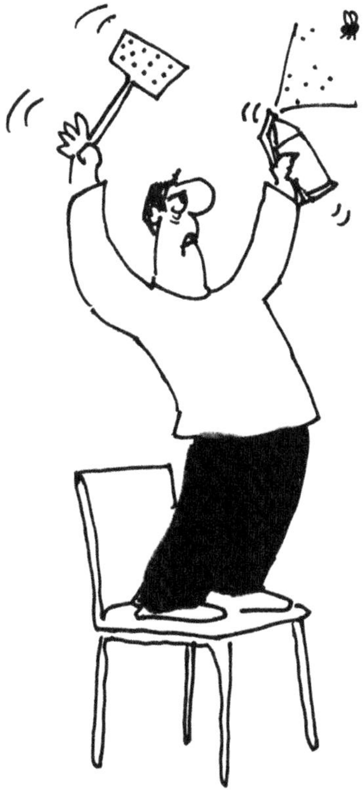

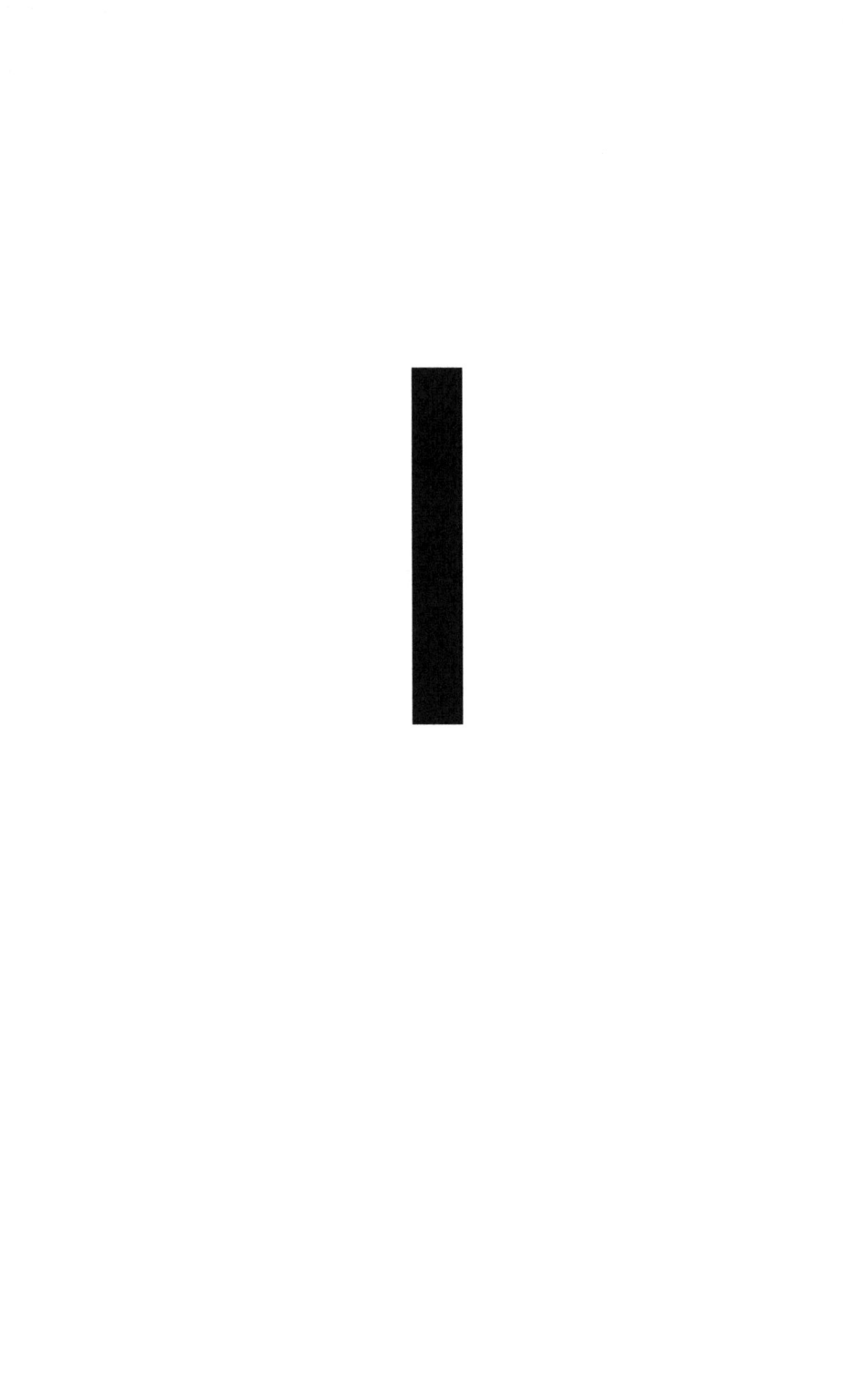

Iconic

Unless it's an object worthy of veneration, no it's not. When something is described as iconic what they're really meaning is…it's quite notable…worth a second glance…possibly even one of a kind...maybe even 'Instagrammable'. But an ancient representation of the Holy Family it probably isn't.

'I'm good'

Well, you might well be. Bully for you. Or more kindly – I'm glad. But please can we drop the habit of offering that as a reply to the question, 'How are you today?' It simply begs the question in response, 'Good at what, exactly?' And therein lies the start of a tedious semantic argument – well, only tedious if unlike me you don't find such things mildly entertaining.

Inaccurate packaging terminology

'Easy opening' must be one of the most misused phrases deployed by people responsible for designing the packaging with which they seek to destroy our hold on reality. Have you EVER met anyone with the kind of fingernails that make that concept workable? The French are no better: I guess that the phrase '*ouverture facile*' must represent some obscure tradition of Gallic ironic humour, dating back to oral traditions when 'difficile' and 'facile' were easily confused by the average Frenchman.

Inappropriate Americanisms

Unless you live somewhere like Noo (which everyone else should pronounce as rhyming with *ewe*) Yawk, the deployment of Americanisms is affected and to be deplored. This side of the 'pond' – another tedious affectation – we don't perambulate on 'sidewalks', ride in 'elevators', or put our trunks in the 'trunk', for example. And if you mean to say, 'I couldn't care less', please don't create unnecessary confusion by saying, 'Like I could care less', goddammit!

Inappropriate familiarity

'What can I get yer mate?' Setting aside for the moment the obvious ambiguity, is there any more dispiriting welcome in a pub than this sort that you can typically expect from some oik who bizarrely sees himself as some kind of social equal or, worse, chum. Look mate, I'm NOT your mate, have no desire to be, and it's highly unlikely I ever will be.

It's the same with the uninvited use of Christian or first names by, for example, people in the NHS. I well remember my late mother-in-law, who wasn't normally much of a stickler for formality, being aghast at being addressed by a perfectly civil GP as Enid, even though she was vaguely acquainted with him. 'Do I know you?' she demanded, in her best Lady Bracknell 'a HANDBAG?!' manner.

Inappropriate use of the present tense

What IS it with presenters, even on supposedly serious subjects, and even in the case of supposedly serious talking heads that they say stuff like 'About this time, Queen Elizabeth the First is getting a bit batey'? She might well have been getting a bit batey five centuries or so ago – but STILL?! How does THAT happen?! This ham-fisted commentary technique only serves to make me – well, tense.

Incompetent wine pouring

I've lost count of the number of times I've been in a restaurant and the waiter who's just arrived at the table to pour the wine manages to drip it all over the tablecloth in the process. Even on occasion a supposedly pukka sommelier. It is surely one of the key skills of a waiter – and indeed, ANY civilised human being – to be able to twist the bottle gently and lift slightly as the pouring stops, so that there are no drips? A bit like the expertise I acquired on archaeological digs as a teenager, whereby you flick a shovelful of earth onto the distant spoil heap, dropping the shovel at the last instant so that the muck flies through the air in a cohesive clump rather than a scattering of detritus which has to be cleared up again. (Though I confess I never quite mastered the art of driving a heavily loaded rear-wheel-steered digger, sending one over the edge of a ten-foot deep trench – not to universal applause, as the crane-hire costs to retrieve it pretty much blew the budget of the whole project.)

But back to wine – and ANOTHER thing! WHY does one so often have to demand of the sommelier that he pours enough wine into the glass to actually smell/taste it, rather than nine times out of ten the mingy quantity that barely covers the bottom of it? Even if it's a half-decent claret, it's not as if he's dispensing nectar of the gods with a preciousness beyond the comprehension of ordinary mortals, from whom it has to be shielded.

Ineffective toasters

In much the same way as you encounter teapots that don't pour (*see* Vol. I), it always seems to me extraordinary that decades after its invention (actually, well over a century, by a Scot by the name of MacMasters, I gather), the chances are that the toaster you've just purchased will be barely fit for purpose. And it will of course immediately upon arrival *chez vous* enter into an unholy alliance with your smoke alarm, whereby whilst resolutely refusing to carry out its toasting duties it will at least generate an ear-splitting screech on a daily basis from its partner-in-crime.

I am fairly confident that either the aperture in your newly acquired shiny toaster won't be wide enough to allow for a decent slice of bread to go in – or weirdly, come out once it's been toasted (on the assumption that it slid in there reasonably easily in the first place) – or that one side of the heating element will be stronger than the other, so you never get evenly browned bread. Or that the pop-up mechanism isn't good enough to completely jettison the contents on completion (it's NEVER like in the cartoons, sadly, where the toast flies across the kitchen). You then find yourself jamming a knife in for all the world like a miniature crowbar to get at the toast which by now is starting to burn, when you end up snagging the knife in those red-hot little wires, thereby cutting the lifespan of the damned thing to a few more days at best.

And – crumpets, eh?! Has ANYONE ever managed to get a raw crumpet into a toaster, watch it toast satisfactorily, and then emerge without so much as a whimper? At college back in the day, we had a far more adroit methodology, which consisted of winding paperclips onto the bars of a gas fire and jamming crumpets onto the sharp little ends. Perfection. Unlike, of course, those fatuous mini-conveyor belts you encounter at naffer hotels, where you watch for maybe ten minutes until a warmish slice of unbrowned bread eventually falls out, so late in arriving that your 'full English' has gone stone cold in the meantime.

Infantilisation

I'm not sure whether this word exists, but it definitely should, to capture a particularly annoying twenty-first-century phenomenon. Whether or not it's related to the new 'boomerang kids' (ugh) syndrome, whereby no one is expected to grow up before they are in their thirties, or with WFH, or from absurd levels of child protection that preclude anyone from taking any kind of risk whatsoever (with the possible exception of bungee jumping) until they're about to start drawing their pension, there is undoubtedly a problem with preventing people from maturing. I've stopped following my college's Instagram feed because it is so puke-inducing in this direction, with students who are almost too old to have fought in the trenches being cosseted to a degree that is simply peculiar. But then in a world where seemingly middle-aged people skateboard, drink from 'sippy cups' and wear onesies – not generally simultaneously, thankfully, though nothing would surprise me – maybe I shouldn't be questioning this.

Instructions

How IS it that, almost without exception, anything you buy that requires more than a simple press of a button comes with instructions so complicated and so incapable of understanding that you begin to doubt the obviously inaccurate results of that flattering IQ test you took all those years ago? These are often accompanied by an exploded diagram that bears little or no relation to the item you're about to assemble, and you resign yourself to several hours of misery ahead, lost in the fog of incomprehension. And it almost goes without saying that these are invariably printed in the smallest font obtainable, against grey, and so compounding the difficulty for anyone aged over sixteen. And that's before the issue of 'lost in translation' rears its head.

Now in any case, any self-respecting Englishman is honour-bound to ignore any instructions, so this is all really of little consequence. That is, until you've finished assembling whatever it is only to find there are some bits left over which should have been incorporated in Step 3c. So THAT'S why the damn thing looks skew-whiff – and always will. Bookshelves will never be truly horizontal; wardrobe doors will never close properly; and the barbecue will forever look slightly drunken (which will of course fortuitously not get noticed, seeing as it will always be surrounded by people in a similar state).

See also Flatpack furniture, People who seem incapable of following simple instructions

Insurance companies

I very much doubt that I can be the first to draw attention to the unappealing symmetry in the relationship between insurer and the insured, namely that, informed by generations of experience of this unhealthily symbiotic relationship, each believes the other to be entirely crooked in attitude and behaviour. So, in the same way that insurance companies' wretched small print too often enables them to wriggle free from their responsibilities, too many policyholders are inclined to inflate the value of the items declared as lost. I'm guessing, as a consequence, that if you actually work for an insurance company you live your life in a state of perpetual confusion, your moral compass continually swinging from pole to pole, leaving you bereft of any sense of where exactly you stand. Well, if you WILL work in the insurance sector, I guess you get everything you deserve…

Intentional obtuseness

Don't you hate that blank-faced expression of manufactured miscomprehension that sometimes meets the meekest of queries?

By way of example, let me explain that the southwest of France, where I have spent a lot of my life, discarded the Saintongeais dialect a couple of centuries back – and that the natives, being French, speak French. But you try asking for a chocolatine – one of these puffy breakfast-time viennoiseries – further east on the Côte d'Azur. '*J'ai qu'un pain au chocolat,*' was the response when I last tried this, the implication being that she hadn't the foggiest idea that the two things are identical – and no doubt come en masse, ready-to-heat, from the same manufacturer. So I grudgingly accepted the put-down and the chocolate-filled croissant, resisting the urge to correct both her grammar and her attitude.

It can be much the same further north in France. In oh-so-posh Deauville I once had the temerity to ask – clearly in the accent of a '*pluc*' from la France profonde – for '*une carafe d'eau, s'il vous plait*'. The waiter, who presumably had spent much of the last couple of decades serving up jugs of water, peered at me pityingly, uncomprehending. After a couple more tries, my accent becoming more and more Parisian with each attempt, my bizarre request was finally understood. '*Ah, une carafe DE L'EAU!*' he exclaimed. Tosseur.

But please do not think this only applies to France. Have you ever had that experience when you're in a carpark and have just glimpsed a free parking space to your side as you pass? Well of course you stop and start reversing gingerly, all of four yards, let us say. At which the driver behind adopts a horrified expression, as if to say, 'What is this MADMAN doing? Is he trying to kill us ALL?! What CAN have possessed him to try such a LETHAL manoeuvre – and us with a baby on board too? He, of course, has never had such an experience himself, it being such a rare occurrence, so cannot imagine that you are in fact undertaking a very simple, utterly inoffensive, totally explicable action which doesn't really call for him to clasp his forehead in disbelief and eventually drive past muttering expletives.

Invitation

See *Invite*

Invite

When did the word 'invite' cease being a verb and become a noun? I bristle whenever I see or hear it used in that way. If it weren't so clichéd I'd use the word egregious to describe its misuse in place of the perfectly adequate word that is already in the lexicon: 'invitation'.

See also Egregious

Irish theme pubs

Proper Irish pubs in IRELAND: very acceptable. Anything that pretends to be one in another country, very much not – any more than the Guinness in such an environment is likely to be. Out-of-place Irish artefacts, Irish-style music, graphics, pictures/photographs, Celtic malarkey all point to the likelihood of a thoroughly dismal experience – the total opposite, in fact, of a good 'craic'.

It is, of course, very similar whenever you encounter an 'English pub' in some benighted location overseas, such as a dusty retail park on the wrong side of the strip in Las Vegas or in the basement of some ghastly chain hotel. In an effort to replicate what its owners forlornly believe to be the genuine article, you will as like as not encounter battered deep-buttoned chesterfields (when were they EVER found inside any self-respecting pub?!); fake book-backs glued to the MDF; moulting stuffed animals; and a stack of boxes containing family board games. Never a trace of bar billiards, darts or skittles, and obviously no chance of a properly kept and piped ale. Under the circs I'd rather take myself off to an unpretentious if tasteless (as like as not in every sense) diner, which will at least be 'real'.

J

Jeans with slits, tears, rips etc

Can ANYONE explain why people can't simply wait for their jeans to start wearing out, choosing instead to pay over the odds for a new pair which have been artificially distressed, so much so that it's only the occasional stud that's holding the damn things together at all? I know many people are inclined to suffer for the sake of fashion – I give you Manolo Blahnik spikes, whalebone corsets and bound feet, by way of examples – but can ANYTHING be as uncomfortable as a pair of jeans in which the legs consist almost entirely of chafing threads of straggly denim? I guess it's all in the name of over-exposure, which has been touched on elsewhere in this and the predecessor volume – but, nobbly knees and wobbly thighs? I'd rather not be confronted by those uncovered, thank you all the same.

Look, they don't have a full pair of jeans between them.'

K

Kafka

See French bureaucracy

Kafkaesque dealings with remote, cold-hearted, uncomprehending corporate monoliths

There is a peculiar sense of overwhelming helplessness to so many of one's encounters as a consumer with big business. I can only really describe it with reference to *Das Schloss* and *Der Prozess*, which is remarkable when you consider that these works were written something like a century before one could only deal with entities like internet service providers, telecommunications companies, insurers and airlines and the like remotely. How prescient was Franz Kafka in describing the miseries of call centres and the refusal of their denizens to accept that you might have a point – if indeed they deign to take your call in the first place.

And how much more 'relatable' would his books have been if he too had had to start a court action against a telecoms company (whose brand name repeats two common letters) for them to accept that one wasn't lying; or persuade another (brightly coloured) one to accept that I hadn't wilfully cut my own phoneline but that – not entirely coincidentally – the 'engineer' who'd visited that very day might have had something to do with it; or threaten the chairman of a now long defunct insurance company with a media campaign to publicise that they were not paying out what was due after six months of failed exchanges. I could go on. And have…

Kids

Perfectly reasonable word when used in the context of goats. Otherwise to be avoided. I was once on *Woman's Hour* (don't ask), and attempting to draw the distinction between baby goats and small children predictably failed to gain any traction. 'Down with the Kids'; 'Kids Television'; 'Kids Entertainment'; 'Kids Room'. Drr – WHY? I am still engaged in an 'industry' in which perforce the term 'Children's Entertainment' (as in 'Children's Hour', for those with long memories) is outlawed – as, sadly, too often are apostrophes (and when they are deployed, you can safely bet a million dollars they will be in the wrong place…).

The youngster?... oh she's watching kids' television with the Nanny

L

Lavatory paper discarded at a beauty spot

First, apologies for the 'beauty spot' cliché, but it's unfortunately appropriate for this particular issue. What IS it that compels so many people – the world over, as far as I can ascertain – to perform a substantial lavatorial function in an attractive sylvan location AND THEN LEAVE THE EVIDENCE BEHIND to fester for the best part of a decade? Surely there cannot be a direct correlation between the attractiveness of a copse or even, God help us, picnic area and the onset of, ahem, an urgent need to evacuate. And why is the loo paper always PINK? If you MUST do it, please at least take the outcome and associated paraphernalia home with you and dispose of it in a civilised fashion. Or use a leaf, prior to responsibly composting it.

See also Litter

Law

See The law

Lazy stereotypes

Where to begin? Or, frighteningly, where to stop? All breakfast TV programmes seemingly have to have a male (he/him, presumably) and a female (she/her, I'm guessing…but these days, who knows) smiling at each other, then the viewer, then looking on admiringly at their counterpart as he/she reads his/her lines from an autocue. And whereas all ads for household products used to feature an Anglo-Saxon husband with smiley-even-if-patently-long-suffering wife (wearing a wedding ring, I had clients who insisted – seriously), and two children (a him and a her…less likely to be something in between a generation ago), two years apart, now if a TV commercial DOESN'T feature someone 'of colour', someone with telegraphed sapphic – or the male equivalent – tendencies, and a child with ADHD it'll never get past the adland legislators.

All football commentator teams now have to include a lady, as do all quiz shows. All cop TV series must include in their cast a cross female senior police-person with a hideous private life, and every murder victim featured in such a series will inevitably be female, young and attractive – and her sad corpse revealed within ninety seconds of the programme starting (probably only partly covered in leaves to protect her dignity). All paedos sport thick glasses with that brown top edge and wear beige and shoes that look like Cornish pasties. All tabloid front pages are still trying to compete with 'Gotcha' all those years ago – and are failing, hence the multiplicity of weak puns which editors mistake for cleverness. All paperbacks on sale in airports have raised shiny type on their front covers and are 'No. 1 bestsellers'. All sales 'must end soon'. Aaaaaaaaarrrggghhhhhhhh!!!!

Leggings

Who can EVER have thought these were a good idea? And why EVER in white? And what compels the most inappropriately shaped people to sport them? And…jeggings?! Yuk! Leggings – NEVER jeggings, to re-confirm – are borderline attractive only on appropriately shaped legs, but the wearer should not be allowed to decide for herself; rather, submit her proposal to a qualified panel of aesthetically shrewd judges, e.g. people like me.

Letting the interests of species like bats, toads and newts trump those of the human race

This isn't so much a clever reference to a recipe from *Macbeth* as a plea for a sense of proportion in our dealings with apparently endangered species. It's not just stately homes and ancient churches that are in danger of being obliterated by an overweening concern for whatever brand of bat happens to be desecrating a much-loved building, rather than the humans who built them and would like to continue in occupancy: anyone who wants to improve their home but finds progress impeded by a colony of self-centred bats or self-important newts is likely to be banned from so much as laying one brick upon another, on pain of extreme punishment. And as the appeals process lumbers on you'll find yourself laying out thousands to some well-intentioned but dim-witted consultant who did a master's in animal husbandry but who doesn't give tuppence for the opinions of the person actually paying for their alternative lifestyle.

Absurd. Over the decades town planners have been permitted to destroy pretty much every decent market town in the country, and yet – find a loathsome but ever-so-slightly-unusual toad in your back garden and you can kiss goodbye to that smart little conservatory you've hankered after. Whatever happened to common sense?! We all know that all the toads will do is happily make a new home in your neighbours' compost, in the same way as the bats will vamoose to the nearest darkened building and the crested newts relocate to a twee little garden pond three doors down. And this doesn't merely apply to the more unattractive denizens of the neighbourhood: just pray that you never encounter a dormouse here or in France or the phrase 'wildlife protection' will take on a whole new significance in your no doubt already-complicated life

Lightbulbs

See Far more different kinds of lightbulbs than can really be necessary

Litter

I well know – and after fifty-plus years of sailing absolutely get – that the rubbish that is slowly destroying the world's oceans is one of the chief concerns *de nos jours*. But this whinge is about the garbage issue that is, literally, closer to home. I've been banging on about the modern-day curse of litter since I was first in long trousers. I mean, just, WHY? Why chuck a fag end out of the car window? Why decorate the hedgerows with dog-poo bags? Why are the verges of our roads festooned with single-use plastic drinks bottles? For what reason are laybys adjacent to bluebell woods always thought of as the perfect final resting place for a soiled mattress? And why are our pavements besmirched by countless millions of gobbets of discarded chewing gum, that by all accounts has a similar half-life to plutonium?

See also Lavatory paper discarded at a beauty spot

Oh hi...I'll call you back we're looking for a beauty spot to dump some litter

Lived experiences

Experienced readers will already be aware of my intense dislike of tautology (and self-evidently of exaggeration), and this is merely one of the newer ones in common – I use the word advisedly – usage. Obviously, we've all had experiences (not all bad, I trust) and we have all lived (if only in some cases, only a little). But please spare the rest of us by NOT sharing your 'lived experiences'. One or the other will do, ta everso.

See also My truth

Long-stay car parks

Who ARE these people who manage to get one of the parking spaces that's a civilised distance from the pickup bus stop?! I always seem to end up in something like Row Z73, a half-hour's trudge from the stop. But there ARE people who contrive to find a gap in Row A: what is their secret? Do they loiter just inside the barrier for twenty-four hours watching for A1 to become available, rather like the sad souls who queue overnight in sleeping bags waiting for the start of the Selfridges sale, in order to bag the star bargain of a 60-inch LED TV at a silly price?

Mind you, there's one more thing in a long-stay carpark that's supremely irritating – thinking you've found a space miraculously in Row N, only to discover once you've started reversing into it that there's the world's smallest car hiding behind the comforting bulk of a Land Rover Defender next door. Meantime, you realise that whilst you've been cursing your luck the bloke who was originally behind you has just bagged a space that really was a space only five cars up, and so you resign yourself to being relegated once again to Row Z.

M

Madrigals

Look, these may have been acceptable as light entertainment in the sixteenth century, but puhlease…no more 'hey nonny no' and all that in ours. It's basically just a load of over-excited shepherdesses and men with uncomfortably high voices (and presumably uncomfortably tight trousers). As for glees – oh, for God's sake (I assume the category name was intentionally ironic, since they induce the opposite reaction in me). There's only one close-harmony malarkey even worse – Barbershop Quartets. Yuk. Too many candy-striped waistcoats, fixed grins and finger-clicking for my liking: an anti-aesthetic experience if ever there was one.

See also Morris dancers

Male washrooms

No they're not.

Mamils

Just as the wrong sort of female shape isn't best served by leggings, so the majority of – probably paunchy – middle-aged men aren't best advised to venture outdoors in body-hugging Lycra. I can speak with some authority here since (a) I'm male, (b) I'm sadly beyond middle-age, (c) I cycle, a lot, and always have done and (d), again sadly, I'm not exactly svelte. But when I pootle out on my bike, I don't do it in the kind of clothes that are less forgiving than the sort of skin-tight bodysuit that made Catwoman so – ahem – interesting, back in the day. And SHE didn't have lumps and bumps in the sort of place that your average MAMIL tends to flaunt when he lopes into the pub. By and large, it's unlikely to be big – and it's anything but clever. And as for that saggy arse malarkey…

See also Leggings

Mansplaining

The verbal equivalent of manspreading (see below). I completely get that it can be tedious and patronising, but have you noticed that there doesn't seem to be the female equivalent, as in 'womansplaining'. This will often take the form of a talking-to on the subject of why, oh why don't men do emotion; the need for every journey to be accompanied by a plethora of luggage items (including things that haven't been used in a decade but might come in handy); and why the washing-up from a dinner party has to be done before bedtime, not midway through a Sunday morning (surely that's what Sunday mornings are for – well, that and a perfectly poured G and T, obvs). On a related matter, I've touched on the subject of rearranging the contents of the dishwasher in the previous volume.

But enter the world of 'mansplaining' and it's a territory fraught with pitfalls. True Story Warning (you know who you are, if you're reading this, which I admit is unlikely…): How NOT to seem to be mansplaining when an inappropriately overconfident and supremely under-qualified lady marketing executive comes onto the set on which you're about to shoot a series of TV commercials and complains that the rooms you have created to look like a modern-day upbeat home are WAAAAAYYYY too dark – when the accurate answer is that you've yet to flick the switch on about 100 gigawatts of lighting to bathe it in a warm luminescent glow? Answers on a postcard please (but don't rush: I've retired).

But I'm sure I'm not alone in having had to do mansplaining to MEN too. I once worked on a film with a very highly regarded director, who turned up to a basement edit suite in darkest Soho to check on what Americans like to call the 'colorization'. He hadn't been there more than a few moments before he started complaining loudly about how poor our work was and how it was inconceivable that his precious little film could be this DARK. It was left to me to suggest that he remove his sunglasses and try looking again 'through fresh eyes'. Cue muffled laughter and an atmos you could cut with the proverbial knife. Not a happy session – but a memorable one. We haven't spoken since.

Manspreading

Hey, I'm a bloke, so if even people like me are thoroughly weary of the expansionist policy pursued by 'manspreaders', then God knows how girls must feel. What IS it with some guys on public transport that they feel they have to open their legs so widely in a peacock-style display of manliness that they're in danger of splitting not just their trousers but their undercarriage? They can't ALL be hung like Errol Flynn, and be in need of additional territory into which they can 'expand', surely? Ugh.

Maps, on which, wherever you are, you are always on the fold or the edge

How can this possibly be? It doesn't matter whether you're in the UK or abroad, this is a universal truth if like me you still enjoy map-reading as an adjunct to the Google Maps function on your mobile. Only years of self-training as a commuter with no elbow room, when broadsheets were broadsheets, has given me the skillset required to accomplish the adroit degree of folding that is invariably necessary to 're-centre', as the satnav jargon now has it. Hey – but you try refolding it back to the way it was afterwards. Hah!

Medicine cabinets

See Unruly medicine cabinets

Menus

See Bad menu translations

Milk in first

If you MUST have milk in your tea, you really should be aware that it is anathema to pour milk in before you upend the teapot. It is commonly thought that the distinction between MIF and TIF is a class one, but there is actually a sound historic reason for the alternative methodologies: some centuries ago, when owing to its relative scarcity fine porcelain was not to be treated lightly, putting milk in first meant reducing the risk of breakage resulting from the collision between boiling hot tea and precious cold porcelain. Is that really a consideration in the typical twenty-first-century household? More than that, by following tea with milk, you can gauge the strength of the tea beforehand and adjust the quantity of milk required according to your taste.

Look... over there...!!
They're putting the milk
in before the tea!!

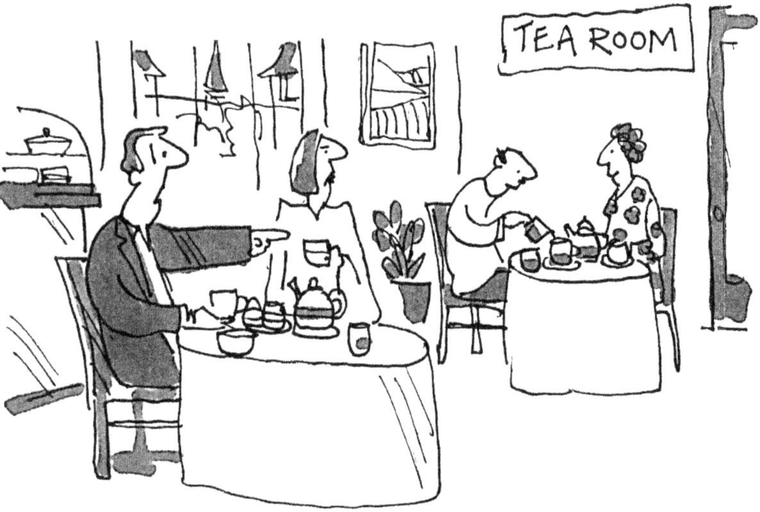

On which note, I will never forget that many years ago, on a visit to Great Yarmouth on a typically feeble summer's day – and I accept perhaps somewhat kinkily – we decided to take tea on the beach. We collected it from a very civil urn lady working in a little hut on the promenade, already 'prepared' in a thick dull-green china jug, ready milked and sugared, and, of course, totally undrinkable. It was one of life's formative experiences, and I hope that my diligent spadework spares my readers from having to endure similarly unnerving knocks at the 'university of life' (the remedy, inevitably, was to retreat to a nearby establishment where a pint of Adnams – an altogether preferable brew – happily pretty much banished 'bad tea memories').

So – are you to be a MIFFY or a TIFFY? Both sound dodgy but it goes without saying (despite the numerous words that precede these on the subject) that TIF is to be preferred.

Mispronunciation of English words on foreign public address systems

Profoundly irritating, unless it's the sexy girl's voice on the bus between the two terminals of Nice airport, who excites you with the prospect that the next stop is 'Our anus'. Oh, the bathos when you realise she trying to say *Arenas*, which to be honest is a bit of a dump.

See also Bad menu translations

Modern-day child and baby contraptions

Not so long ago, I was decanting various grandchildren from the car when I realised I hadn't a clue how to untangle the baby buggy. Now, contrary to the impression you may have formed from reading this book, I am not entirely impractical, but I spent several minutes trying to work out how it unfolded. Fortunately, a youngish parent, realising my predicament, came to my assistance and opened it up, just before all hell broke loose in the back seat. You may imagine the suffering I endured when it came to closing it up again after we'd had a walk.

But it's not just buggies: how MANY variants of the in-car bucket seat for infants can there possibly be? And why is every one so devilishly difficult to install – and that's before you get to the point of actually installing an infant in one, with all sorts of complicated straps, buckles and fastenings that would do credit to an astronaut securing himself into a rocket from the Apollo era.

These devices of course are NOTHING compared with the hideousness of the travel cot! They come into your possession all neatly folded, with the mattress support wrapped tightly round in a bear hug, and it's only when the grandchild's arrival is imminent that the dreaded moment can no longer be postponed: you must now put it up. If you've ever experienced this, you'll be able to picture the next half an hour vividly. The supposed instructions printed on the mattress support have all the usefulness of a history of the charitable works of Saddam Hussein and are twice as long. You find that the back and front of the damn thing seem to lock into place quite easily – and then maybe even one side. Hurrah! But the fourth side of the rectangle resolutely refuses to do the same, so you disassemble it and start afresh – over and over and over again. And then suddenly, just as you're about to cede defeat, for no apparent reason it all clicks into place.

Even so, you spend half the night in a cold sweat, semi-convinced that it's all going to collapse back in on itself, with the precious grandchild trapped and wailing, and its parents in a state of a total unforgiving for days – weeks – to come. But no, miracles of miracles, it has stayed intact, you discover. Moments later, your small hard-earned glow of satisfaction quickly starts to dissipate as you begin to realise, horror of horrors, that before long you'll have to pack it all away again…

Morris dancers

Nooooooooooooo!!!!

See also Madrigals

Moths

Now I grant you that certain species of moth have a gorgeousness about them that belies the havoc they're capable of wreaking (and I don't know about you, but seeing hundreds of long-dead specimens pinned in a display case always induces a strong sense of ennui, not to say sadness), but I can't be alone in despairing of the repeated damage done to carpets, jumpers and other woolly items by their depredations. Apparently, there's now a plague of the blasted things. It can't ALL be down to overuse of central heating, or climate change or the extinction of most of their natural predators (hang on – I thought that was US?!), but I'm damn sure that the abolition of proper old-school mothballs has something to do with it. Speaking for myself, I'd risk a hint of camphor in my life if it meant that my jumpers could at least be worn more than once.

See also Insurance companies

My truth

Surely, 'my version of events'. Which may well be different from someone else's. Truth, surely, is only something that can be independently verified and objectively described. Like the speed of light, perhaps, or the temperature of water at boiling point, or the ghastliness of ramblers coming into a pub with their walking boots swathed in plastic bags and then only ordering complicated soft drinks in a phenomenally drawn-out fashion whilst you stand behind them, empty pint-glass in hand, suffering from the effects of advanced dehydration.

See also Lived experiences

N

Name badges

What is more self-important than a nonentity at some ghastly trade fair flaunting a large plastic badge with their name emblazoned on it? Only one thing: continuing to wear it once the event is over, especially 'out on the town' later. The Croisette in Cannes is always knee-deep in the ghastly things, the year round, it seems. What MUST the locals think? And who wants to know anyway? And then some people go and compound their grating self-importance by stuffing the pouch which carries their credentials with as many other people's business cards as possible, as if to say, 'Look at me…not only am I insufferably pompous, but see how many wretched people who have had to put up with my attentions in the past couple of days'! Wankers.

Nausea-inducing fried eggs

I read somewhere that oriental types first began eating hens' eggs something like 7000 years ago, so you would have thought that by now the human race would have mastered the simple art of frying the damn things in such a way that they both look and taste, well, appetising.

So how is it then, that more often than not, on a spectrum from hideously undercooked to absurdly overdone, they're NOWHERE NEAR the bloody middle! Now I really like eggs – fried, boiled, scrambled, poached, as an omelette, coddled, even – but I can't be alone in almost gagging when a fried egg is produced with that semi-see-through glutinous stuff coating the topside. And don't give me that American nonsense about sunny side up or over easy: OF COURSE, it should be sunny side up.

To get the perfect result, whilst it's gently frying, simply use a teaspoon to occasionally drizzle hot oil from the pan over the in-danger-of-offending part, until it has 'set', being careful not to stray over the yolk, which must naturally remain runny. Wahey – fried egg heaven!

At the other extreme, steer well clear of those rubbery ones beloved of hotel buffet breakfasts, which to all intents and purposes might have been prepared sometime in the last century, and closely resemble those cute little Haribo versions but without their tastiness. Simply inedible, even in the throes of the heaviest of hangovers.

Needing to pee when skiing

It must be time for someone to invent for skiers the kind of pee extraction equipment that astronauts must surely use. Can there be anything worse than the business of bursting for a leak, having clumped awkwardly sideways downstairs in some alpine bistro, only to find that the time it takes to open an aperture is – how do I say? – near-fatal. There are so many layers and zips and buckles and belts and braces…

Well actually, I HAVE endured worse. The first time I went skiing was in the era of all-in-ones, and I had, to put it politely, a stomach disorder. Of the down-below variety. Every time I managed to get to the bottom (sorry) of a green, then – praise be! – a blue run, I had to make a dash for the conveniences in the nearest restaurant. Which, inevitably, meant buying a glass-of each time. I'm sure my divine instructor (with whom I was ever-so-slightly in love, as well as in awe of her abilities) was convinced that I was, even more than most skiing Brits, a total alky as well as a complete hypochondriac.

Nests of tables

Superficially practical and useful, but in essence just wrong. It's partly the name – implications of infestation – but also partly the way they cluster in rather too tidy a way. It's just not natural, in the way that an occasional table somehow is. I guess like all slightly contrived pieces of furniture they have their day in the sun and then go on to make the occasional appearance in something like *Bargain Hunt* or a twenty-second-century edition of *Antiques Roadshow*. Speaking for myself, I'm still waiting for the 'telephone seat', through whose invention a family acquaintance of little taste but masses of chutzpah made squillions in the sixties, to make a comeback.

Net curtains

Without exception, hideous. Especially those ones with 'designs' incorporated rather than just made of plain semi-opaque material. And even worse when grubby, as they almost invariably are. I was once told that all those yellowing ones in London government buildings were there to afford some kind of protection in the event of a blast that blew in the windows. Fair enough, I suppose, as a justification, but they could at least wash the bloody things.

Nibbles

NO!!!!! Canapés – yes. Snacks – just about yes. Nibbles: only borderline funny when intentionally confused with 'nipples' in an attempt to defuse the inevitable social embarrassment with humour. Hoho. Recently, the French phrase '*apero dinertoire*' seems to be

Ah nipples... er... sorry nibbles

gaining currency, and whilst it is undoubtedly an improvement on nibbles, it brings with it a strong note of affectation. Let's just stick to a bowl of pork scratchings and be done with it.

See also Grazing

No-platforming

All the progress that mankind has made since the onset of the Enlightenment is in danger of being undermined by so many recent changes in attitude, notably the absurdity which is 'no-platforming'. Until not so long ago this was the kind of experience met by long-suffering Waterloo commuters through gritted teeth and a retreat to the cabin bar for a restorative tincture while the powers-that-be decided how and when to find a berth for the 18.37. Now, sadly, it has an altogether more sinister meaning, as foolish, weak-minded people choose who might or might not be able to deliver a lecture, sermon or speech in the debating society, on the grounds that they may get upset by something that is said. What utter, utter nonsense – but of course it has the potential to be far more deadly, being just one step away from book-burning. Do I sound cross? You betcha!

See also Cancel culture, Content warnings

0

Officialdom

See X-ray airport staff

Omnipresent yobbishness

I can remember my parents banging on in the sixties about mods and rockers and antisocial transistor radios as if it were yesterday. So yobbish behaviour is nothing new – and I'm pretty damn sure that the Flemish artist Pieter Bruegel the Elder knew exactly what I'm banging on about when he depicted bad behaviour in paintings such as *Wedding Dance in the Open Air* back in the sixteenth century. Check it out – especially the leering chap in the red 'troos' in the left foreground if you don't believe me. So it's not a new phenomenon, then, nor a particularly British one. But isn't it now more omnipresent – more 'in yer face', as it were? I blame TV dramas such as 'Stenders for encouraging it, as well as social mobility – or at least, mobility, so that yobs these days aren't confined to their own ghettoes but rather have the means to invade yours, whether this is your local high street on a Friday evening or the departures 'lounge' (dread word) of pretty much every UK airport. And whatever you do, avert your gaze as you pass a primary school gate on any day in term time, lest you come across hordes of parents sporting their velour pyjamas…

Ostentatious physical exercises

Why can't people keep their P.E. to the privacy of their home or the sanctity of the gym? Parading your pathetic scrunches, jerks, planks, squats and so on in public is just – well, pathetic. I've seen people lunging at airports and even doing star jumps in the street. AND in Lycra. Bloody hell – gives a whole new meaning to the phrase physical jerks. And if you must warm up, please do so in your bedroom – not in the bus queue, where the potential for nauseating your fellow would-be travellers is overwhelming. I blame those boot camps and the ever-grinning Joe Wicks.

Out-of-reach parking machines

So you've manoeuvred your car close enough to just about reach that payment machine at the carpark exit, causing a couple of hundred quid's worth of damage to your precious alloy wheels in the process. Then you reach out, only to find it's still tantalisingly distant. Aha! You try to loosen your seatbelt – that'll do the trick – only to find it's done that locking thing, so you have no choice but to unfasten it completely. Out you lean. Nope, still no joy. With a grim inevitability you resign yourself to opening the car door, only to bash it against the wretched machine because you're TOO close for that particular action (Bang! There's another fifty quid to go on making-do before you hand the car back to the lending company). Nothing for it now but to reverse, get out, walk over to the machine and complete the transaction that way. Only by now, there are two other cars queuing behind you. Goddammit! And you can't get out of the car because the door is jammed, so you start your flashing lights, begin reversing gently, perhaps give a little hoot on your horn, at which point the psychopath at the wheel of the car behind becomes apoplectic – nothing like this of course has NEVER happened to him, so he just thinks you're, well, insane.

This, of course, is a classic Basil Fawlty moment – the kind you often witness involving a British vehicle at a toll station on the French motorways on the day of the 'grand depart' – seventy-three irate Frenchmen will within minutes have accumulated behind it, torn between relishing the foreigner's discomfiture and raging at the ruination of their holiday plans by the extra two minutes delay in their journey.

See also Intentional obtuseness

P

Painting

See Painting a fence having taken the trouble to check the weather forecast, only for the heavens to open just as you're finishing

Painting a fence having taken the trouble to check the weather forecast, only for the heavens to open just as you're finishing

This, of course, is a classic sod's law situation, made all the more annoying because repainting a fence that now has a coat of oil-based paint mingled with rainwater is harder work than preparing and painting the damn thing in the first place. And here's the other really weird thing: how often when rain is forecast do we suddenly experience a day of unbroken brilliant sunshine? Odd.

Pairing

Not what you might think, which would be way more interesting, nor a reference to an arcane Parliamentary practice. This is about getting your phone to talk to your – or indeed, any – car's media system, your tablet or even your central heating boiler. Even if your device is in 'pairing mode', as like as not it will resolutely refuse to do the deed, for all the world as if it were one of those standoffish giant pandas that's been shipped to a zoo halfway across the world simply to indulge in a bit of productive pairing but chooses instead to lounge about sucking on a bit of bamboo.

Paninis

By all means have a panini in Italy, but do we HAVE to have them inflicted on us in the UK? What is wrong with a proper toasted sandwich, using traditional low-quality sliced bread, made in the traditional, slightly sleazy way? Or even in a Breville.

Paper cuts

How is it that something as inoffensive as a piece of paper can inflict almost as much pain as a direct hit from an anti-aircraft shell? And for REAL pain, forget the tiny slice into your index finger: how about the incision on your tongue caused by licking a gummed envelope?

There's only one thing more excruciating – slicing yourself open on a blade of wild madder in the garden. Think you're too manly to wear Teflon-coated garden gloves? Think again: have YOU ever grasped a madder stalk to yank it out and watched in horror as it stays firmly put, leaving rivers of blood flowing from the wound it's left gaping on your fingers? And you KNOW both that the cut won't heal for days and that you'll get scant sympathy because it looks so innocuous.

Why is life so bloody unfair?!

Pebbledash

There are few sights more likely to lower the spirits than an otherwise perfectly serviceable 1930s suburban semi covered in what looks like hard cold porridge. Why would anyone do that? And please don't think you can get away with kidding us it's OK

Of course I won't ring 999...
it's a bloody paper cut!

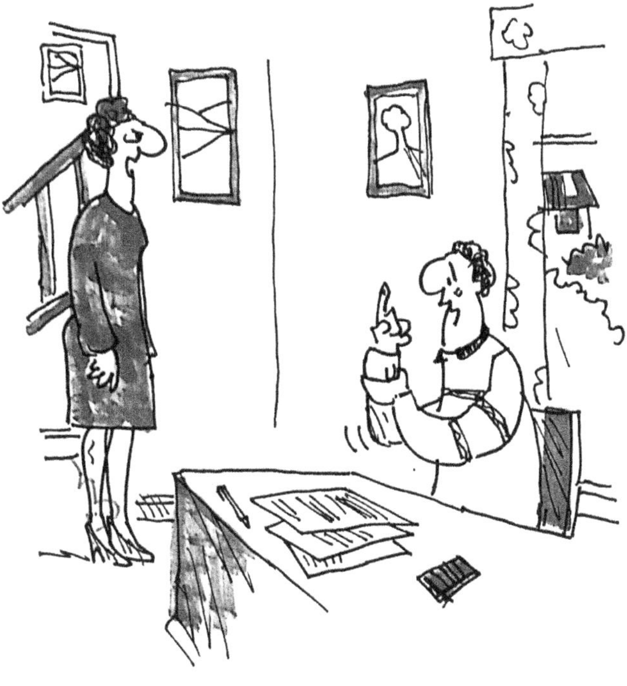

by painting it the colour of Windolene. It's very much not OK – OK? Give me a good expanse of honest-to-goodness reddish London Brick – or maybe some solid Cambridge Whites – but do us all a favour and demolish your house if that's the only practicable solution to pebbledash embarrassment.

People who go to fancy dress parties without bothering to wear fancy dress

No, it's not 'ironic': it's lazy. Seriously. Someone has gone to a huge amount of trouble to come up with an imaginative and original theme such as 'Superheroes' or 'Vicars and Tarts' and the very least you can do is to humour them by entering into the spirit of things by wearing a pair of fishnets or some such. Or don't go. Simple really.

People who seem incapable of following the simplest of instructions

Anyone who's ever installed a loo with a macerator in their smallest room will know exactly where I'm going with this. For the uninitiated, this type of lavatory has a very small exit pipe, so the egress of the contents is assisted by a macerator, which – yuk, sorry – mashes up what you've left so that it is more easily 'digestible'. Unless they're a full-on masochist, everyone who has one of these puts up a little sign saying something like: 'On no account put anything inside this bog that has not passed through you'. What, I ask, could possibly be clearer?

And yet…and yet…

I've lost count of the number of times I've had to rediscover my inner plumber and sort out the vile-smelling disaster that ensues when this simple instruction is disobeyed. Large quantities of toilet tissue are a problem, but the worst offenders – I'm sorry, but it's true – are items of feminine hygiene. The last such event was beyond me, and cost close on 600 euros to put right. So, at great expense (approx. 2000 euros since you ask), we replaced this vile contraption with a proper flushing loo, and I now sleep easier at night.

To be fair, though, accidents do happen. I'm sure one of my sons won't be too embarrassed if I recount an episode from when he was about ten years old, on holiday in France. He'd managed to get his member caught in the zip of his trousers, which necessitated a trip to the doctor, who applied a small bandage. This was bad enough, but when he went to use it the next day, forgot about the bandage, which fell into the loo. He, of course, pressed the flush…and the rest, as they say, is history. I for once had had the good sense to stay in London so managed to avoid the entire ghastly experience. For his part – in a manner of speaking – he wore his boxers back to front for months afterwards. Understandably. The lasting psychological damage has yet to be fully evaluated, but physically it must still work since he is the father of three…

See also Instructions

People with no taste

Life – and, obviously, this book – is too short to do justice to this enormous subject, but I'm including a few examples just so that you know I'm not ignoring this vital genre of First World problems.

I've lost count of the times I've been to an impressive restaurant in France, with an equally impressive wine list, only to hear a voice at the next table demand a *jus d'ananas*. I'm sorry…but what's THAT about?! What dish has ever been created for which pasteurised pineapple juice rammed full of preservatives is the perfect accompaniment? I guarantee that if such an item is to be found, it will come in a small jar with a plastic screwtop lid with a brand name which could not be more appropriate for the tasteless consumer: LOOSA. I kid you not.

On which note, who buys a brown Ferrari…marries white stilettos with black tights…has soap on a rope hanging in their shower…displays a box of tissues inside the rear window of their car…sports those peculiar and enormous 'black hole' earrings… has a pair of fake (and suspiciously perfectly spherical) bay trees either side of their front door…or gives their home a kitsch name like 'Sunnytrees' in place of a respectable Number 43?

I know I run the risk of sounding like a latter-day Nancy Mitford, but she was in her heyday almost seventy years ago and maybe it's time that her vital work on 'U and Non-U' was updated – although whilst I'm with her on 'the sofa', so to speak, why one was supposed to refer to a chimney-piece rather than a mantelpiece thoroughly defeats me.

See also Piercings etc etc etc etc

Perennial unpunctuality

I'm pretty sure that the exponential growth in unpunctuality is in direct correlation with the growing prevalence of mobile phones, enabling the user to be late with impunity, secure in the knowledge that, whatever happens, contact can easily be made – to proffer an excuse, to rearrange, or to blame. And occasionally, even, to apologise.

Perpetually disrupted picnics

It is axiomatic that the moment you spread out the chequered tablecloth on the grass – and, inevitably, even before you've had an opportunity to weigh it down with all the paraphernalia of a proper picnic – that a Force 7 gust will whip into a frenzy and send your tablecloth into the nearest hawthorn bush and your companions to the safety of the car. Surely there's a new 'old weather lore' phrase just itching to be coined, along the lines of, 'once yer gingham tablecloth's on t'grass, t'weather's sure to be a pain in the arse'. Over to you amateur McGonagalls to improve on this.

Pettifogging rules

One of my prize possessions is a letter from the Cambridgeshire Constabulary from roughly a half-century ago, summonsing me to appear before the beak on several charges involving a bicycle. They decided to drop the headline offence of being drunk in charge of a bike (to be fair, due to my condition and the absence of any brake pads, I'd actually ended up in the crotch of the local copper, a rather excellent, long-suffering fellow, known to generations of undergraduates for his general forbearance), and instead booked me for not having a rear light visible from a distance of fifty yards. Naturally, I declined to appear – or more accurately, forgot – so I suspect I'm still a 'person of interest'.

I recount this happily ended (to date) tale only to flag up the absurdity of so many rules in our society. Who decided that we may not run on the escalators of the London Underground? Did you ever knowingly elect a government – or even a councillor – who pledged to introduce sleeping policemen with abandon?

Why doesn't Instagram permit the baring of nipples? Who first came up with the dread phrase, 'Have you paid and displayed?' And still rankling, nearly sixty years on: why weren't long trousers allowed at my grammar school until the second year…and why did we have to wear school caps until we did our O-levels?

I assume that a fondness for pettifogging rules is what motivates someone to want to be a librarian…or a traffic warden…the person who composes the endless Ts and Cs on a typical website… an airport X-ray attendant…or, dare I say it, a school prefect.

Picnics

See Perpetually disrupted picnics

Piercings

For generations, male gypsies were known to wear a gold ring in one ear to pay for the cost of their funeral. This is a very rare instance of a practical purpose to a piercing. All other manifestations of piercings in the male are to be abhorred, and indeed the majority of those in the female. Do your ears REALLY need to be festooned with a bewildering variety of adornments, or a hole drilled through your earlobe, like those primitive natives in some far-flung jungle that used to be the stock-in-trade of *National Geographic* magazine? People in your high street will be wearing those dinner plates in their mouths next, or maybe lengthening their necks by means of a dozen hula hoops or some such. And does your tummy button, front bottom, mouth, nose, cheek or even breast bone need to have a hole drilled in it so that you can dangle something of dubious aesthetic value from it? I think the test is simple: if you're a girl and have a piercing in the lobe of each ear for a tasteful earring, fine. If you're anything other than that, or are fiddling with a different part of your anatomy, then very much not fine. I hope that's clear.

Pillows that do the opposite of what nature intended

The standard dictionary definition of a pillow is 'a rectangular cloth bag stuffed with feathers or other soft materials, used to support the head when lying or sleeping'.

In respect of far too many pillow-type contrivances that one encounters at bedtime may I offer the following, more accurate and much less ambiguous definition: 'a semi-hard block of indeterminate materials, disguised in a bag, which is a pain in the neck, both metaphorically and literally'. Or in layman's terms, 'a breeze block'.

Armed with this understanding, you will be less likely to be disappointed by what is almost certain to welcome you at the head of a strange bed, even in some of the better hotels and homes. Don't bother trying to mould it into a form which offers even the faintest possibility of a comfortable night's sleep. Without hesitation chuck the sorbo rubber-filled sack (at best) or sandbag (for that is what it most resembles) onto the floor along with the weird strip of material that so often lies across the foot of the bed (for what reason no one has ever satisfactorily explained, by the way: who invented THAT, for pity's sake?). Then carefully fold any spare clothes you may have, origami-style, into a rectangular pillow-type shape – preferably with a cotton shirt acting as the outer – and hey presto, you have the equivalent of a pillow that is far more likely to be conducive to sweet dreams than what you were originally presented with.

Oh, and if you're in France, you can even forget the word 'rectangular'. Square, maybe, or oblong, or cylindrical, but seldom rectangular. Just saying.

Plastic bags in supermarkets that want to remain as a single sheet of double-ply plastic rather than allow themselves to open up and serve a useful purpose

How is that you can struggle for fully five minutes trying to open out one of those super-thin plastic bags at a supermarket – especially, natch, those ones you typically find on the fresh veg display – whereas the checkout girl manages it in a nanosecond, whilst simultaneously (tautology hazard warning) multi-tasking? I've seen all manner of techniques essayed – rubbing vigorously where you think the opening is; blowing into what you hope is the aperture; attempted tearing; trying to establish a fingerhold where the bag handle will eventually be; silent cursing; not-so-silent cursing – but by and large you might just as well as try to open it up where the damn thing really IS sealed, viz the bottom of what will eventually be a bag. Please write in with your most effective solution to this syndrome.

Plastic netting containers for shop-bought fruit and veg

Please…WHY?!

Plugs

See The British three-pin plug

Pool robots

When these work, they have the capacity both to entertain (how does THAT work…where will it head next…how does it climb the wall…?) and clean your pool. But more often than not, they don't. You've checked the water pressure, taken it apart, stroked it lovingly, pulled the hose this way and that, dropped it at first carefully and then angrily into the water so that it sits on the bottom…and then it just sits there and looks back at you balefully, as if to say, 'You really expect me to do another four hours' work, underwater, AGAIN?!' We even had one with a pair of stick-on eyes that gave the impression it was looking where it was going. Which was fine, until I saw it heading towards a small pile of detritus and swerve to avoid it. Not just once, but over and over again as it did its rounds.

In the end, almost invariably you give up, and resort to being your own poolboy, beavering away with the manual vacuum at the end of the long pole – not quite the same as lounging next to the pool with a negroni watching whilst a machine that cost a few hundred quid scurries about doing the work. Weirdly, of course, though nothing has changed, the next time you get the robot out, it works, first time. What's THAT about?!

Popular culture

Surely the ultimate oxymoron. Reminds me of the excellent phrase, 'There's more culture in a pot of yoghurt than there is in Birmingham.' And on the subject of oxymorons, I'd find it difficult to beat this headline I once saw in a magazine: 'Six delicious lentil recipes'. Be glad to hear of your favourites.

Potpourri

What's the point? It's invariably just an expensive bowlful of dried bits and pieces that's been dunked in some artificial fragrance and whose environment-improving potential is dissipated three days after its opening, after which time it just sits there accumulating dust for the best part of a decade. A bit like the fad for those little sticks in a pot of gunk that everyone had in their bog for a while, that were supposed to 'freshen' the atmosphere but actually ended up just looking like a few little sticks in a pot of gunk, contributing nothing to the atmos of the smallest room – no matter how many times you turned them upside down.

Printers that prompt suicidal thoughts

As soon as you're confronted with that absurd enjoinder on your screen to 'find printer', you know you're in for hours of misery. I've already 'found' it, dammit, on the table next to my laptop – why the hell can't the laptop see it?! As like as not you'll now find yourself downloading yet another bit of software replete with pages of Ts and Cs, and I swear that if the word 'smart' is involved it can only be in an ironic sense – smart software in my book is up there with 'army intelligence' as another of the ultimate oxymorons. Let's for a moment indulge the fantasy that your computer starts talking to your printer (though in all probability that's AFTER another trip to the wretched computer store to buy a special cable because the two devices have decided that they can't have a wireless relationship), and in all likelihood you find some absurd new feature on your laptop called something like a 'garden', inviting you to indulge your creativity with the bloody thing.

Now I may be alone in having this attitude, but if I want to be creative I'll pick up a paintbrush or go and sit at the piano: almost invariably all I want my printer to do is to print something out uncomplainingly, probably in black and white, one-sided and on something as conventional as a piece of A4 paper. And then, when I want to repeat the process a day or so later, I'd rather like the desktop to be able to find the printer without hours of interrogation and to simply follow my instructions.

Of course, in the meantime, the relationship between the two supposedly inanimate objects will have been irrevocably disturbed by your rash decision to use the scanner feature, with the result that it has gone on strike and the only effective remedy is to chuck it away and start all over again. It is at this point that you realise that the horrendously expensive print cartridges (gallon for gallon one of the most valuable commodities in the world today) and the one-time-use-only cable that you bought don't fit the new piece of kit, and you're struck forcefully by the logic back in the eighties of every decent-sized company having a print-room where a dedicated – and I mean that in every sense – team would manage the infernal machines on your behalf. *O tempora, o mores!*

Q

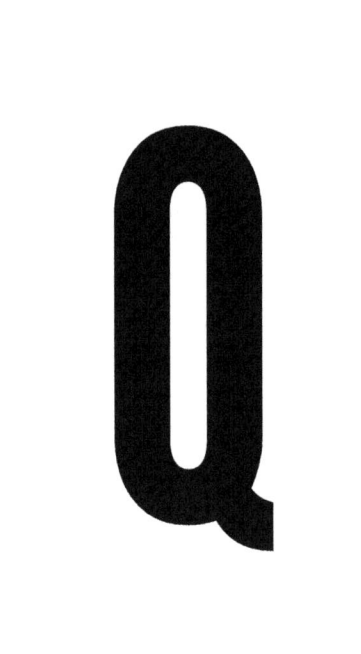

Queues

No matter whether it's a queue for passport control, a cashier, a ski-lift, a check-in counter or supermarket checkout, what superior authority designated that YOUR queue – however much shorter it superficially appears to be – will be the one that moves slowest? You can almost guarantee that at least ONE person in the queue ahead of you will not have the correct document/money/pass/loyalty card and/or will want to talk about anything from the immediate transaction to the possibility that intelligent life exists elsewhere in the universe. Well, not in YOUR case, obviously. But whatever you do, don't try queue-hopping in desperation, because (a) you will then encounter human life at its most aggressive and ugly and (b) the queue you just left will speed up whilst your new one slows down, with the result that you will (a) be made to look a complete wally and (b) come to question some of the other life choices you have made, and which looked so promising at the time. My advice? Take a book (preferably this one) and try to let the experience wash over you.

R

Red ropes outside wannabe in-demand venues

It is axiomatic that the less in demand a venue is, the more substantial the red ropes outside restricting entry. In fact, there's probably a direct inverse correlation to be drawn between the undesirability of a venue and the extent of red 'ropage' outside. And don't you hate the flourish with which a third-rate doorman lifts the rope aside when someone whose 'name is on the list' arrives?

Relentless spam emails

Now I know you're going to say I bring it all on myself with my questionable internet browsing, and therefore have no one but myself to blame for the incessant filling of my inbox with all manner of digital detritus. But are you REALLY sure about that? What did I ever do to deserve two or three matching pairs of emails a day about 'quick-dry sandals', for example? Moi?! WTAF? And why for pity's sake does the opt-out thingummy never work? I've lost count of the number of times I've unsubscribed to websites to which I never subscribed in the first place. The same syndrome as for sandals (REALLY?!) goes for garden hoses, business loans, drones, zoom cameras, woodworking, and dozens more dreary products. I could drone on – oh, and yes, I've had spam about drones as well.

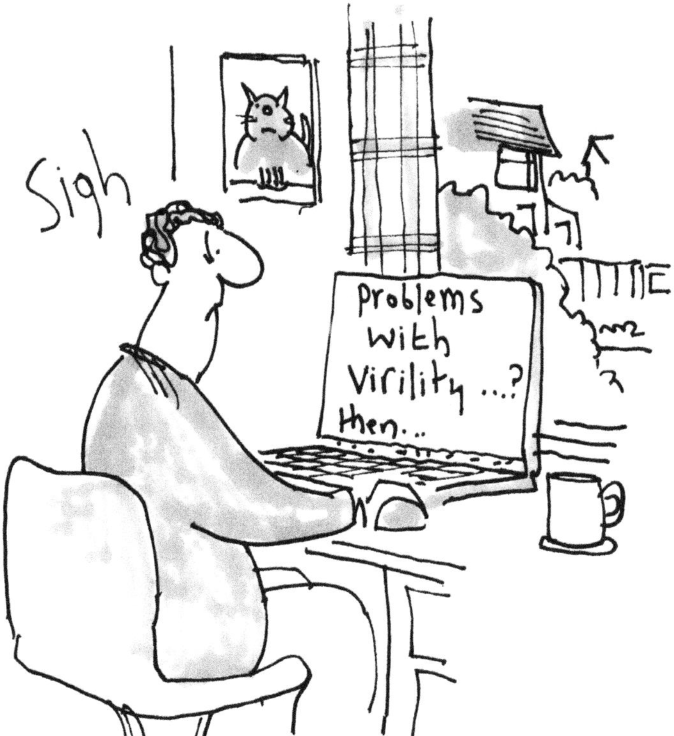
Sigh
Problems with Virility ...? then...

Removing shoes on a plane

What is it that compels people – typically in my experience, unhygienic types to start with – to remove their shoes on a plane? Flights are seldom overheated in the first place, whereas your socks/tights probably are. It's just thoroughly antisocial behaviour – and no: we're not interested in you flaunting your 'creative' socks. Or indeed anything else – on an overnight flight I once witnessed a 'gentleman' get down to his boxer shorts (none too 'decent' in themselves) before turning in for the night. Yuk.

Repeat online purchases which are unstoppable

Oh, how I regret ever purchasing an inoffensive-seeming app called 'Racing Pigeons' to placate a couple of unruly tiny grandchildren. They weren't far off doing Common Entrance by the time I could put paid to it, as it were, and the cost must have run into gazillions. There seemed to be no way of stopping it. The same goes for all manner of repeat purchases, which one thought of as a one-off and then promptly forgot about until a couple of years later when another wodge of money departed the bank account, never to be reclaimed. All manner of services can subject you to this treatment, but the worst offenders it seems to me are things like anti-virus software and credit agencies: oh, the irony!

Replacement bus service

One of the most dismal phrases known to man.

Resto pubs

Restaurants good. Pubs good. Hybrids bad: the worst of both worlds. The pub ceases to be the fount of happiness which its inventors intended it to be, and the resto will almost invariably turn out to be a pale imitation of everything one wants from a restaurant. The creaky barstools will have been replaced by faux-leather 'seating'; the pickled eggs and pork scratchings will have been displaced by 'boil-in-the-bag' fusion foods; and cask ales as like as not will have been discontinued in favour of the inevitable Sauvignon Blancs and bloody Merlots and Malbecs.

There are occasions – well, rather a lot in my case, as it happens – when only a pub will do. There are other instances when one hankers after a decent restaurant. But who in their right minds thinks, 'I know, I really fancy a trip to the local gastro-pub: it's sure to be a thoroughly enjoyable experience…'?

Rolling news

Has anyone considered the effect on the national – or indeed, individual – psyche of continuous exposure to the same old news, 24/7, as the vogueish phrase has it? Especially when two thirds of it consists of trivia, endlessly repeated, not just on the hour it seems, but every quarter. Time was, when the *Six O'clock News* on the wireless was considered enough of an update on the world and its woes. Then came such abominations as the *Nine o'clock News* and *News at Ten*, and its bastard offspring – often with similarly portentous use of Big Ben style graphics and ominous music with too much brass instrument content for my liking. And as if that isn't bad enough, it's all over the airwaves from an unearthly hour of the morning. Look guys, there just isn't enough significant news – or 'stories' as you like to call them – to fill the hours, so why don't you just play some soothing music accompanied by appropriate bits of film to lift the spirits?

Roundabouts

See The way that French people negotiate roundabouts

Rules

See Pettifogging rules

S

Salad on a hot plate

Can anyone explain why, in a restaurant that is incapable of serving a hot meal on a hot plate, they contrive to serve a cold salad on a hot one?! If it's so easy to whip a still-warm plate straight from the dishwasher and plonk the cold food on it, mightn't the same principle apply to food that's INTENDED to be served hot?

See also Bad coffee

Sash windows

Yeah yeah, they look fine in context – typically a good solid Victorian building – but by and large aren't they a bugger? No one's quite sure whether the English, the Dutch or the French first came up with the counterbalancing sash, but whatever, they surely can't have had as part of their seventeenth-century patent application, 'a device designed to render near-impossible the cleaning inside and out of the glass whilst maximising the potential of every small draught to enter unobstructed'. How MANY dedicated homeowners have run the risk of death or serious injury by hanging outside their window either upside down from the top half or downside up from the lower in a vain attempt to reach that last inaccessible corner with a squirt of Windolene?! Give me a good old casement window any time.

See also Secondary glazing

Secondary glazing

Hmm. Best read in conjunction with the note on sash windows, above. The precursor to modern-day double-glazing, but still too often inflicted on totally innocent homeowners by busy-busy inspectors who insist that listed building regulations will not permit anything else by way of insulation – 'anything else' not being in the spirit of whatever period the building dates from.

On that note, by the way, I was strangely relieved to learn that this attitude is not a uniquely British phenomenon. Staying in the famous Arne Jacobsen-designed Royal Hotel in Copenhagen, I was bemused by the appearance in our room, minutes after our arrival, of a maid bearing an armful of large fresh towels. Assuming there was some mistake, I tried to shoo her out, only to be told that she was there to line all the window sills with a thick layer of towelling to prevent the ingress of water when the predicted heavy rain arrived, as I think it always does in Denmark. Apparently, the authorities wouldn't let them replace the useless award-winning windows in this twenty-storey block with anything that might actually keep out the elements, so they had to resort to more primitive methods…on a daily basis.*

But back to secondary glazing. Apart from its invariable sheer hideousness, how many of you have ever mastered the business of cleaning it inside as well as out? And even if you can manage to lift the damn panels out of their little gutters to get at the reverse side, how do you EVER get them back in again? None of the problems presented in *The Crystal Maze* have anything on the challenge this represents, and so the wretched double-glazing will inevitably repose against the back of the garage wall for eternity, leaving the grotty guttering behind as sort of naff trim, forever reminding you of your general incompetence.

*This will no doubt instantly remind any Cambridge history student of a few decades ago of the multi-award-winning faculty building on the Sidgwick Site, which was invariably unfeasibly hot in summer, unbearably cold in winter, let in water when it rained, and continually dripped condensation (in a LIBRARY, for God's sake!) in all other climatic conditions.

See also Sash windows

Self-assembly furniture

See Flatpack furniture

Self-important gins

Time was, when a gin and tonic was a merely a satisfactorily straightforward, comforting precursor to Sunday lunch. No longer. And it's not just the tonic that's got overcomplicated. Every day seems to see a new gin launched at a not-very-expectant market, each with its own newly invented heritage and an increasingly desperate collection of botanicals to give a dubious point of difference.

It's simple, really. You just want a good quantity of a decent dry London Gin with a hint of juniper about it, in an unfussy glass with the same amount of a proper orthodox tonic water, a decent quantity of ice, a couple of slivers of lime (and if you're picky, a bit squeezed in), and Bob's your uncle. Chuck in a few dried juniper berries if you must, but I swear you won't notice the difference (unless one gets stuck in your teeth). All else is vanity.

Selfish – or should I say, lethal bastard – cyclists

Full disclosure: I'm a cyclist of some sixty years standing, or sitting mostly, and I've done the odd turn of speed.

But.

This would have been on a road – not a pavement, a footpath or a towpath. And I wasn't clad in luminous go-faster Lycra with my legs shaved, wearing a helmet that wouldn't disgrace a time-triallist on one of the Grand Tours, and with my ears blocked by earphones blasting out a zillion decibels by The Darkness or some such. Guys…and yes, they usually are guys…do us all a favour and stick to going up and down Box Hill till you drop, and leave the gentler spaces to people to enjoy without being in fear of their lives.

See also Mamils

Self-tangling wires

So. (Apologies for this lapse: *see* Vol. I). You've installed the TV, DVD player, satellite box, sound bar, hi-fi (are they still called that?) and internet hub. You've probably added an occasional lamp and a charging cable or two for a couple of personal electronic items, hem hem. You may even have poked a few through that little Velcro band that in theory will keep it in some kind of order. Except, of course, that it won't. EVEN IF NO ONE TOUCHES THE INSTALLATION FOR A YEAR, you KNOW that when you next look there will be a ghastly spaghetti-like tangle of dust and cobweb-covered cables that for all the world look like the interior of one of those 1950s telephone switchboards you see in an Ealing comedy.

HOW DOES THAT HAPPEN?! Your other half swears they haven't been near it. You know you haven't. The cleaner blatantly never looks behind or underneath anything. And yet…and yet… A bit like in *Toy Story* there must be some kind of secret life of gadgets that sees them come to life and intermingle in a thoroughly inappropriate way once the lights are out. I'd be glad to receive any other plausible explanations.

Serviettes, paper

Nothing wrong with the product – it's just the word that makes me feel nauseous. They're paper NAPKINS. It doesn't matter that they're not new-fangled: the ancient Chinese used them for tea ceremonies – but I bet they didn't call them serviettes. In fact, a little research (OK, Wikipedia) tells you that their word was *chih pha*. And why do buffet organisers persist in that thing of dampening them, then wrapping them tightly around a knife and fork, so necessitating your tearing it off – and inevitably shredding it – with your teeth before you can start eating? And what's that 'paper art' thing all about, when they are used in some origami-style activity before you sit down at your table, leaving them entirely unfit for use as originally intended?

Shared tables on trains

I suspect that most hardened commuters never voluntarily sit at one of these, which invariably entail aggressive games of footsie, as their owners jostle for advantage, for all the world like getting entangled with Vinnie Jones on a football pitch in his 'crazy gang' heyday. And even if the leg space tussle gets settled relatively amicably, with a grim inevitability you then have the table space confrontation, which I've known to last as long as two hours. The weapons of choice in these low-level disputes include laptops – and the angle at which the screen is bent – mobile phones, newspapers, magazines, coffee cups, wallets, purses, and 'snacks'. And even though it should be transparently obvious that each of the occupants has a semi-formal allowance of space immediately in front of them, it is extraordinary how so many try to squeeze in an extra few square centimetres over and above this – often in a rather sly way, maybe looking into the middle distance while their hand slides a possession into unoccupied but spoken-for territory immediately opposite or adjacent. It's redolent of those neighbour disputes, when one's fence creeps a metre or so outwards over a period of time, until they've gained an extra width of garden with a market value of half a million. Profoundly irritating.

See also Manspreading

She/her and all the other similar abominations

I'm sorry, but this is ALL bosh, isn't it? And this whole business of someone referring to their newly-non-binary offspring as 'they' for fear of causing offence just serves to show that people don't have enough really significant things to be concerned about. Why don't you try living in Afghanistan, or the Ukraine, or North Korea and then see what life's priorities really are?

Sherry, sweet

See Sweet sherry

Signs

See Absence of worthwhile signs amongst a forest of unnecessary ones

Singing loudly at concerts

See The person next to you at a gig singing so loudly that you can't actually hear the performer you've paid almost £100 and queued for four hours to see

Skiing

See Needing to pee when skiing

Sleeps

Just about acceptable, for example, in the context of renting a cottage ('Sleeps four'), but this word's use otherwise tends to make me a bit sick in the mouth. 'Mummy, there are only ninety-six sleeps until Christmas!' 'Only fifteen sleeps till we go on holiday, wahay!' Oh, for heaven's sake: it's the number of days you're counting, if you must, not the number of times you hit the sack.

Smart motorways

No, they're not.

Smoked salmon packaging

How do some people produce those dainty wafer-thin slices of smoked salmon from a package, when I invariably end up fiddling with a gooey clump of the stuff? How do you work out which side of the sliver is protected by that little sheet of cellophane? Is there a YouTube video someone can point me to?

See also Badly packaged bacon…prosciutto…salami…etc

Sneezing

See Dramatic public sneezing

Snowboards

A contraption invented by the devil to ruin enjoyment of the slopes by proper skiers. NB 'grey boarders' are especially to be avoided, but please take it upon yourself to admonish anyone who uses the misleading and unhelpful phrase 'greys on trays' within earshot. The sound of an out-of-control boarder from behind careering in a straight line down the hill towards you, a proper skier – out of your sight line – is one of the most terrifying sounds in the known universe. Bloodcurdling doesn't begin to describe it.

Sofas with bits that tilt

Whereas a La-Z-Boy is just about understandable and not uncomfortable, a sofa (or 'seating unit') which contains moving parts is not. Especially when made of faux leather – or 'pleather' as I'm reliably informed is the term. And TBH I'm not really sure about real leather in the context of a three-piece suite, but let's not get distracted. Back to moving parts, this is not just on account of the dubious aesthetic but also its strong association with the concept of the couch potato, which is uncontestably contributing to the national malaise. Lying is for bed or people whose grasp of the truth is dubious, not for the living room.

Soundtracks in toilets

Setting aside for the moment the sheer absurdity of playing ANY soundtrack over the PA system inside a toilet, who on earth decided that playing recordings of snippets from literature over the sound system whilst one is peeing was a good idea? If I hear Alan Bennett in his campest of coy Northern accents recounting the exploits of Toad in The *Wind in the Willows* one more time, I SWEAR I'm going to throw up – and miss the bowl, for good measure… It's become a feature of self-anointed upscale hotels to indulge in this bizarre behaviour: if it's not Alan Bloody Bennett, it's some superannuated actress reciting *The*

Lady of Shalott in portentous tones, for God's sake. WHY?!?!? I've now gone off Tennyson FOR EVER. By the way, is it just me who could never understand why it wasn't Lord Alfred Tennyson rather than Alfred, Lord Tennyson – or was he just being awkward? Just asking.

See also Best practice, Chocolates on pillows

Spam

See Relentless spam emails

Spanish food

Yes, I know that some Spanish places do cooking that is 'world-class', whatever that means, and I've eaten in some phenomenal Spanish restaurants, but by and large you really have to work hard to find somewhere that doesn't dish up cooked potatoes that are too cold and salad that doesn't contain half a can of sweetcorn and a load of warm crushed tuna that you weren't expecting to accompany your 'ternera'. And 'revuelta', as the name implies, is simply revolting, unless you've a hankering for a damp plateful of tepid scrambled eggs mashed up with bits of prawn.

Most important of all, although strictly speaking beer isn't a food, your lager is NEVER cold enough, which explains why the first basic Spanish phrase I learned to recite many years ago was – and still is the most important in the language – *Una grande cerveza con dos cubitos hielo, por favor.* You know I'm right. Just make sure you wolf it down before the ice melts…

Staycations

For those of a certain age, the summer of 1976 will linger long in the memory. It was an extended period of extreme heat and drought in the UK that led to the appointment of a Minister for Hosepipe bans and, more importantly, was one of the very few occasions when gentlemen in the Stewards' Enclosure at Henley Regatta were permitted to remove their blazers (but sadly not the underclothes of the young things which accompanied them – well at least not until darkness fell).

As an object lesson in why to avoid staycations it would be hard to beat my experience that year. Having suffered the commute into London all through summer in temperatures often in the high thirties, we chose to holiday in Tintagel in mid-September. It rained pretty much all of every single day, with the effect that the wood we gathered to light the fire in our rented stable was so sodden that it needed a gallon of high-octane petrol before it would pathetically and briefly flicker into life in the grate. All our limited resources went on purchasing anoraks, jumpers, wellies, woolly hats and hot chocolate. Never again, we vowed.

And, of course, nothing has changed. A staycation offers a Hobson's choice between endless traffic jams, crowded beaches and disputes with the 'pay-and-display' machines if the weather is benign, and endless traffic jams, windswept beaches and disputes with the 'pay-and-display' machines if the weather is vile. On this basis, even the ghastly process of getting in and out of Stansted Airport looks almost attractive as an alternative, sandwiching as it does the likelihood of a fortnight somewhere where the weather is reliably good and the 'pay-and-display' mentality has yet to take hold.

And it's not just the British seaside that I'm talking about. For this keen hillwalker, the delights of a few days traipsing across

High Peak or up and over Scafell – the horrors of the motorway system notwithstanding – have to be offset against the near-certainty that you will be confronted with howling gales and driving rain, unless you leave booking until the last moment and have a reasonably firm forecast for a few days' relatively bearable conditions. Even then it can go wrong. I once pitched a tent in a field near Edinburgh with no rain apparently in prospect, only to be woken in the middle of the night with a thunderous downpour battering the canvas. Tentatively, I unzipped a couple of inches to peer outside, only to discover a herd of cows all around me, some of which had decided it was the perfect spot on which to relieve themselves (they were clearly taking the piss, ho ho). It's only if you have had such an experience that you realise quite how capacious is a cow's bladder. Staycations?! I think not.

Steak served in a restaurant that bears no relation whatsoever to the style in which you ordered it

'Quelle cuisson, M'sieu?' is a question asked by French waiters to which the only acceptable answer obviously is either saignant or à point. Or if you're a true masochist, maybe bleu. But no matter, whatever you specify, the chances are it'll turn up from the kitchen in whatever state the chef decides is appropriate. The added bonus in the States, of course, is that it will also taste of next-to-nothing and be an unrealistic shade of garnet, in the same way as farmed salmon is invariably a totally faux version of pink. Oh for the days of the long-lamented Berni Inn, when a steak was a steak and they knew how not to cook it, if you get my drift. Oh, and dish up an old-school 'schooner' of Fino to whet your appetite.

Stereotypes

See Lazy stereotypes

Stupid car names

I'm not talking here about the names which some owners give to their cars (WHY my parents' first Hillman was called Lancelot I will never know), but the absurdly silly brand names sometimes given to cars by their manufacturers. Why 'Lodgy' on the rear-end of a Renault, I wonder? Unless they meant it to be 'dodgy' and it got lost in translation, which would at least have been apt. And why on earth the Citroen 'Jumpy'? Maybe that was meant to be the more accurately descriptive 'lumpy'. Happily, I once saw an example where pasted just underneath the word 'jumpy' was the name of a hire car outfit called… Titi. Oh, how we larfed. Haven't they heard of sports bras? And who, apart from my wife, bizarrely, can have thought that the Fiat 'Lounge' would be an attractive concept? There was once a Toyota 'Deliboy', believe it or not, but then the Japanese have a knack for such things – as in the Honda 'Dunk', the Nissan 'Homy' and the ironically named Mitsubishi 'Carisma'. Then of course, you have the brand names which translate unfortunately: I give you the MR2 which in French sounds like sh★t, which is a relatively accurate moniker for this particular brand of Toyota, for example. There's something of a syndrome for car-marketing types to beware of here, for the Rolls-Royce Silver Shadow very nearly became the Silver Mist, which in German refers to what the French know as *merde*… something of a theme going here.

Super-excited

No you're not. That's just something people say on LinkedIn when in the past they'd have said, 'We're pleased to announce…' And I doubt very much that you're 'passionate' about dogfood, bog rolls or bathroom fittings either, if that's the sector you've landed a job in (although I guess you might reasonably be about lingerie): you're possibly motivated – probably by your remuneration 'package' (there's another ghastly HR word for you) – which would be understandable if not particularly praiseworthy.

Super-hydration

If you were tussling against Rommel in North Africa with the Eighth Army, the need to keep hydrated was probably – and properly – fairly uppermost in your mind. But if all you have to endure is a few stops on the Central Line, or a gentle jog of a few miles, do you REALLY need to keep adequate water supplies WITH YOU AT ALL TIMES?! For pity's sake, even the public service announcers on our transport systems have taken to adjuring us to ensure that we drink enough water. As someone who enjoys skiing and sailing, where in both environments you're surrounded by water in one form or another, it is axiomatic, not to say ironic, that keeping hydrated is moderately sensible, though diluting H_2O with something faintly medicinal like pastis or whisky always seems like 'best practice' to me. But in normal everyday life… I mean, GET A LIFE!

    Not long ago, in the course of a series of medical examinations, the Rhodesian – sorry, Zimbabwean – nurse who was dealing with me advised that I should drink five – yes, FIVE – litres of water a day for the good of my health. Hmm, I said, that presumably includes the water content of things like claret, lager, tinned tomatoes and the like, otherwise I'd be in danger of drowning. She assured me that, no, it had to be in its pure, unadulterated form. Needless to say, she turned out to be totally mistaken and this nonsense was debunked in due course, and I now mainline alcohol on a daily basis just to ensure that my water levels remain at an appropriate level.

See also Constant changes to dietary advice

Swear words

See The sad decline in the use of proper English swear words

Sweet sherry

An abomination, obviously, esp. if the dread word – in this context at least – 'British' is inserted – or 'Cyprus'. Manzanilla aside (or, as an understandable substitute, a well-chilled fino), the only other acceptable form of sherry is in the style of Pedro Ximénez, so self-consciously sweet and treacly that it can only be served as a digestif or as the lubricant for a sticky pudding. The obvious pairing in this instance is for pre-prandial drinks to include a chilled white port – the drier, the better, self-evidently. In this way you will rather satisfactorily be zigging when the rest of the world is zagging.

T

Tailgating

It's bad enough seeing the whites of your OWN eyes in the mirror – but someone else's, at 90 mph, eyeballing you with all the aggression of Mike Tyson in his prime? You're already keeping to a steady 88 mph…there's an endless stream of traffic ahead…you've left a sensible gap to the car in front…and yet Max Verstappen in the beat-up Transit three centimetres from your rear bumper isn't happy. A glare in his direction won't suffice to effect what psychologists term 'a behavioural shift', and it would simply be too wimpish to move over, obvs. The most fun and risky manoeuvre is to dab your brakes fleetingly, but when I say risky – I MEAN risky. Or you can kid him that you're braking by momentarily flicking your sidelights on (as in a thousand car chase sequences), so that thicko THINKS you're braking and loses ground. Ho ho. Aggressive handsignals – that's clearly a euphemism – are probably best avoided. And since you don't have the rear-facing armoury of James Bond's Aston Martin, the best you'll be able to do is put your hazard warning lights on to irritate him. Whatever, this experience will seldom last long, since within half a mile he'll be overtaking you and dodging back into the gap you'd so sensibly left in front.

And now it's your turn…

See also Bloody car drivers who sneak up on your inside before pulling into the sensible gap you'd left behind the car in front

Technology continually making expensive, treasured things redundant

By which I explicitly DON'T mean mobile phone chargers. I'm referring to that huge pile of records (OK pedants, VINYL), lovingly accumulated in your late teens that stills lurks, loved but unused, in the cupboard under the stairs. Not a million miles from those hundreds of CDs that nestle, unwanted, in their neat little shelf stacks, adjacent to the thousands of pounds worth of DVDs that glare accusingly at you when you turn to Netflix. Funny, though, how crossword compilers STILL incorporate the abbreviations LP and EP into so many clues: what era are they living in?!

And, of course, before streaming made them redundant, you ummed and ahhed about chucking out your 8-track cartridges and the dinky little audio cassettes that, oddly, still seem to be used by police interviewers. Or at least they do in *Midsomer Murders*. And…books. Like many of us I possess many thousands, and the thought of culling the collection fills me with the screaming heebie-jeebies. But let's be honest, these days, beyond the aesthetic satisfaction, there's little purpose in owning them: you can get pretty much all you need to know from the bloody internet. Thank goodness you shelled out for this one though…

Teenage spots when you're middle-aged

Why?

Textspeak

OMG can you BEAR the way that so many people text?! And the twee little endings like LOL and OXO? And apparently the woke amongst us – or are those snowflakes? – are now terrified of full stops, because of the passive aggression they betray. I confess to gaining mild amusement from using shortenings like gr8, shd and tmrw but interspersing these tedious words with unnecessarily long ones, in the manner of a second-rate PhD student trying to impress. And including semi-colons and Oxford commas, too, just for pedants' sake. BUT NEVER CAPITALS, OBVS…WAYYYYY TOO AGGRESSIVE.

That horrid concrete section of the M25

You know where I mean, roughly between 6 and 9 looking at the damn thing clockwise – Surrey, Sussex or some such. Suddenly you go from a perfectly acceptable stretch of traditional tarmac and find yourself on the bumpiest, noisiest road surface imaginable. WHY?! It's a brownish-yellow, ridged abomination that's quite unlike any other section of motorway you'll ever encounter – anywhere in the world. The loud humming vibration it produces at anything above 5 mph is almost enough to make you want to seek sanctuary at the vile services area nearby – but NOTHING could be that bad. Or could it…?

Theatres

See Eating in theatres, cinemas and other similarly inappropriate venues

The bad taste of earlier generations

I think I first became aware of this syndrome when doing up the interior of an Edwardian semi half a century ago. We had decided to replace the marble chip 'n' MDF fire surround complete with coal-effect 'fire' with the real thing, something contemporaneous with the house itself. Yeah, yeah, I know – poncy gentrification blah blah…

Anyway, we discovered a place selling just the thing, complete with its little cast-iron grate and tiled aperture, and on talking to the owner of the establishment discovered he'd made a small fortune twenty years or so ago ripping out these delightful contraptions and putting the fake things in their place. And now here he was, gleefully making twice as much again, helping people like us dispose of the fifties monstrosities and reinstall their predecessors!

This example spoke to me of a universal truth, as we went on to dump the avocado bath suite…look for ceiling coving…seek out respectable door furniture to replace the supposedly ergonomic brushed-aluminium versions…and…and – have all new generations largely despised what went on before in the name of improvements or is it just us baby-boomers? I give you ring roads, crazy paving, stone cladding, metal window frames, tower blocks, package holidays, Vietnam, Fray Bentos meat pies, Teasmades…? But what will future generations make of pot noodles, the internal combustion engine, footballers earning £1m a day and bloody Facebook?

The British three-pin plug

Has there ever been an everyday contrivance as hopelessly overcomplicated as the standard-issue British three-pin plug, which came into general usage after World War II? I blame Dame Caroline Haslett, who clearly had it in for generations of DIYers to follow. Is there REALLY a need in many instances to have recourse to three different screwdrivers – and how many of us have inadvertently stripped the enamel from our front teeth in an attempt to bare the end of the wires? And even when you've achieved that, and managed to open up the damn thing, there's that weird business of doubling the negative wire back on itself to jam it into place round the corner; poking the positive one into that awkward little hole under the fuse (which of course promptly falls out and rolls across the carpet and out of sight); and making sure the earth wire is just that little bit longer so it reaches all the way to its home in the furthest reaches of the plug. That's when you find you've got to twist it slightly out of the way of the screw that holds the whole contraption together – and of course, there isn't enough slack. Count to ten.

Counter-intuitively, this is one thing the French actually do better than us: only fair to give them a plug when it is deserved…

The C of E

Once-revered institution that was for centuries the bedrock of Englishness – a largely civilising influence on a populace largely allergic to religious dogma and home to some of the finest music ever created or performed. Now sadly reduced for the most part to the status of custodian of a number of buildings of historic interest and employer of a dwindling number of semi-secular social-worker types. Typified by miniscule congregations of very elderly, permanently slightly cross people, who seem to have adopted a mission to be as off-putting as possible to anyone under the age of sixty who expresses any tentative interest in what might go on in their local church.

To be fair, this isn't restricted to the C of E. A couple of years ago I was showing one of the – very well-behaved, as it happens – tiny grandsons round a historic church in the wilds of SW France, and he was asking questions excitedly…like they do. Some old bag emerged from the shadows and gave us a severe talking-to, so in keeping with the time-honoured phrase we made our excuses and left. What impact, do you imagine, would this have had on an impressionable little boy? Is it conceivable it left him with a lifelong yearning to have more to do with the established church? Answers on a postcard please.

And as for the C of E's absurd activity during the pandemic lockdown (which this institution took absurdly literally), sadly I think this will linger long in the memory of people whose instinctive reaction has long been to support the Church come what may, often in the face of yet another example of abjectly stupid behaviour.

The common cold

Totally and completely pointless. Antisocial, debilitating, unseemly, tiring, overly frequent – rather as its name implies. And for all those decades of 'cold research' and amateurs saying things like, 'Oh, I'm past the infectious stage', no one seems any the wiser now about the cause, origins or means of cure than they were centuries ago. And now, at the time of writing, it turns out that it's a distant relative of the coronavirus bug: it's got a lot to answer for.

The 'eco' setting on washing machines and dishwashers

I assume this is some kind of in-joke from the likes of Bosch, Whirlpool, Miele et al. Whether it's short for ecological or economical, the fact that any cycle on this setting takes easily twice as long to complete suggests to this domestic god at least that there's something funny going here. There's probably a doctoral thesis on the shelves of some seat of learning in the back of beyond on the subject of 'irony in white goods marketing', which we long-suffering taxpayers have probably helped to fund. If so, could we at least be given a précis?

The insurance racket

See Insurance companies

The law

Now look, some of my best friends are lawyers, but since none of you are wilting lilies there's no reason to look away now.

The giveaway about the law is the line famously given by one of the barristers in the Christine Keeler case: *the law and justice are two very different things*. For someone like me – and, I suspect, most people with a reasonably long career in business – that phrase embodies an inescapable and unwelcome truth. At the risk of mixing metaphors, it doesn't matter whether you are in the driving seat or are being taken to the cleaners, the chances are that your case will turn out to be yet another in a sequence stretching back centuries that only goes to underline that not-so-sacred principle. In a nutshell, even if you win, you very seldom will really have won – but you can bet your bottom dollar the lawyers will have done, and that that footling little case you brought that you thought might bring a mild retribution and even, heaven forbid, a small measure of justice, instead produced a transit van full of expensively photocopied documents and a trail of invoices which betray a quality of creativity not usually associated with a grey-suited solicitor.

The near-impossibility of putting children's shoes on

What could POSSIBLY go wrong? Holding the first shoe in one hand, you plonk the child down and invite it to offer up a foot. Inevitably, the foot and the shoe won't match, so you say 'wrong foot' and get the other shoe ready. And what happens next? The child proffers the other foot, and so you find yourself doing an increasingly desperate series of movements, trying to second-guess when the right foot will match the right shoe. This can take HOURS (which causes the intended shoe-recipient inordinate glee, obvs). Of course, the fun stops when at pre-prep stage you're trying to teach a little boy how to tie shoelaces. In one instance, several decades on, we're still at it…

The never-ending difficulties with Airfix

Rarely indeed during my childhood did I come across a peer who'd mastered the technique of putting together a Spitfire kit without the glue stopping the wheels from turning or the cockpit glass from frosting up. Oh, and getting the miniscule brackets that hold the wheels to stop folding up (AKA collapsing) long before the plane was actually in the air. Or in the case of a sailing ship, completing the kit without all the rigging looking like a cat's cradle. And trust me – I'm not completely handless. But what is more than a little dispiriting is that some decades back, entirely predictably, I repeated this experience with my own boys and have now recently restarted this cycle with grandsons. Presumably I'm doomed to experience this anew – and in all probability for all eternity – in the Seventh Circle of Hell.

The Oscars ceremony

Did anyone EVER actually like the Oscars ceremony? A bunch of preening, pampered people looking smug and summoning ever more dramatic false emotions to outdo the person who was on the podium immediately before them. Featuring a cast of thin, angry women wearing too little and posturing unattractively; thickset, shaven-headed 'security' men standing legs akimbo and looking menacing; thousands of TV reporters and their long-suffering crew hoping for a flash of knicker to relieve the tedium; and hundreds of under-dressed D-list 'slebs' hoping to catch the eye of a leering producer. Desperate. And now we've had a 'faux-fight', for Chrissake.

The perils of painting

I'm not talking here about the embarrassment occasioned by showing off your treasured amateurish watercolours only to discover that they're universally thought to be – well, amateurish. No, this is about home decorating. Why IS IT that the paint-roller lifts off half the carefully sculpted Polyfilla with which you've spent hours covering up the crevices in your Victorian dining room? Why is painting corners so infernally difficult? How is it that the only square centimetre of furniture left uncovered by dust sheets is the bit that attracts that utterly unremovable gollop of gloss paint? Why is cleaning brushes so damned difficult? And why does your wife insist that you paint behind the piano, where no one is ever going to see it in half a century, as if you're one of those medieval stonemasons engaged upon cathedral construction who ensured that even the invisible bits were made perfect *in case God spotted them*?

The person next to you at a gig singing so loudly that you can't actually hear the performer you've paid almost £100 and queued for four hours to see

Whilst it's true that some brilliant musicians like Mark Knopfler and Eric Clapton, for example – without casting any aspersions on their phenomenal abilities and star appeal – don't rank amongst the best of singers, that's no reason for the twerp in the adjacent seat to assume that your enjoyment will be enhanced by their own vocal qualities. I really DON'T want to hear 'Layla' or 'Money for Nothing' from the mangled vocals of Kevin from Finance, who's convinced that the only reason he didn't win *Britain's Got Talent* is because he's got acne. Oh, and now he's started playing air guitar, for pity's sake: where's the Green Room?

The price of bottled water

Absurd.

Therapy

There seems little doubt that some kinds of therapy in some kinds of circumstances are completely valid and worthwhile. (How's that for a plonky, catch-all, give-no-hostages-to-fortune kind of a comment? The kind I'm normally allergic to.)

But can there REALLY be a justification for the enormous industry that's sprung up in recent years around the word 'therapy'? I'd wager that there are more people engaged in providing this around the country than in mining coal, though I suppose at least it has a fairly minor carbon footprint by comparison. I can understand that returning soldiers from Afghanistan, for example, needed a bit of proper TLC, but it sometimes seems that you can be diagnosed with PTSD from something as lame as missing the bus, and be provided with a six-week course of full-on psychotherapy at our expense to get over it. I hesitate to say, 'Pull yourself together!' – but there – I've just said it.

The sad decline in the use of proper English swear words

Maybe because we're all supposed to be so damn PC these days… or because most workplaces seem to be largely populated by ladies…or because we're wimpish…or woke…or whatever, but am I alone in detecting a noticeable decline in the abundance of good old-fashioned swear words in everyday discourse?

Now, I accept the inappropriateness of dropping the c-bomb in all but the most extreme circumstances (when addressing a picture hook that steadfastly refuses to adhere to a wall, for example, for no discernible reason), but what about all the others that no doubt hail back to the time of the Venerable Bede?

My introduction to all this came at around the age of five when I spent the morning on my family's building site, in the company of what my father would have referred to as some 'rough herberts'. One of the men – a plumber, inevitably – deployed a word I'd never heard at our dinner table: bollocks. I loved it, and still do, but made the mistake of trying it out on my mother later that day. Suffice it to say, the rest of the weekend passed in abject misery, and I was never again invited to spend Saturday in the company of plumbers, chippies, sparks and so on.

I've since, of course, developed quite an extensive vocabulary of cusses for use in most situations, but find the opportunities for airing them sadly restricted. Offspring for example, I've noted, tend to disapprove when you swear in front of the grandchildren, so it's no accident that several of them take the mick by shouting out 'Gordon Bennett!' in my direction, which is the most extreme language I am permitted to use in their company. They'd love it more if they knew of some of the great man's exploits, which allegedly included drunkenly peeing in a fireplace in front of the guests at a wedding, apparently mistaking it for a urinal.

The way that French people negotiate roundabouts

I am firmly of the belief that one of the most humorous works of non-fiction must be the French equivalent of the Highway Code, but I've not yet managed to get my hands on one. Several life-experiences have brought me to this conclusion, but the one that trumps them all is half a century of observing French drivers as they make their way towards, round, and off roundabouts. It all starts, not with British-style jockeying for position (for all the world like the closing 100 metres of a sprint stage of a major cycle race), but with a strange gradual coalescing of however many lanes of vehicles into one almost static one. Every vehicle in this lane – without exception – will then be indicating furiously, either left or right, but do not be deceived: the direction they indicate will have no bearing whatsoever on the direction they will eventually take when they come to exit the roundabout. The car at the front of the queue will inevitably wait until no other vehicle is within a kilometre, and will then gently ease out into the outside – i.e. the outer circumference of the circle – lane, WHATEVER EXIT THEY PLAN TO TAKE.

Forget the concept of the sensible or the short way round – or even the racing line, heaven forfend – rather like in the Velodrome (as opposed to the Daytona Speedway) but at a quarter the speed, they will pootle round aimlessly at the furthest point from the centre of the circle, indicator lights flashing any which way but sensible, before suddenly diving off when the idea takes their fancy. UNDER NO CIRCUMSTANCES try to do the obviously correct thing, like use the outside lane if you're turning off early or the inside one if you're turning off later: this will cause massive confusion, hot tempers, much honking and Gallic gesturing, which will continue at least until you reach the NEXT roundabout. No problem there, obvs, because YOU WILL HAVE LEARNED YOUR LESSON. This will be useful in all sorts of ways, especially if you come to apply for a *carte de séjour*, when you will be able correctly to answer lessons on such abstruse matters as roundabout driving etiquette, the cheese-first/dessert-first conundrum, and why handball is so much more important a sport than, for example, rowing. Just saying.

The wrong (kind of) trousers

Writing as someone known to sport shorts in appropriate climatic conditions, and unsurprisingly most often seen in long trousers, naturally I fancy myself as something of an expert in appropriate trouser length. Unarguably, the length of shorts favoured by 1970s footballers is wrong on every level – notably evinced in the infamous 'spot the ball' photograph of the era when the ambiguity of the headline was all too obviously illustrated.

Equally, the Baden-Powellesque version beloved of superannuated scouts, members of the Monty Python troupe and, it seems, paedos worldwide, whereby the hem touches the kneecap, should be an object of loathing. Especially when disconcertingly baggy. Isn't it obvious that, in the context of shorts, a happy medium is easily arrived at, whereby aesthetic considerations are satisfactorily married to practical ones?

On the other hand – or more appropriately foot, I suppose

– long trousers that aren't exactly that, i.e. are less than long, are to be deplored. I can just about accept that on the right girl, capri pants can be flattering, but the male equivalent on a tubby sixty-something bloke who's just stepped from a cruise liner? I think not. Especially when there's a drawstring involved. 'Nuff said. And as for those intentionally not-quite-long-enough long trousers that hover uncertainly above the ankle: what's THAT about?! Surly those went out with Teddy boys and Vespa scooters about half a century ago?

I'm sure Peacock's Gentlemen's Clothing Department in *Are you Being Served*? all those years ago would have known that the trouser leg should neatly 'break' on the shoe, and of course, so should we. Know, that is. All one needs to avoid is that inside-leg-measurement malarkey, to be on the safe side.

The wrong regional accents on regional TV stations

Is it conceivable that TV channels in Scotland parade a succession of voices speaking Home Counties RP? Thought not. Then why are they allowed to cross Hadrian's Wall and head down here to inflict their accents on us in London and the southeast? The same undoubtedly goes for Ireland as well. Look, if we're living in Hampshire let us at least enjoy a distinctive Hampshire burr, even if it makes comprehension near impossible, rather than an impenetrable Glaswegian or Belfast accent, heavy with undisguised loathing of our part of the world and everything we hold dear.

Things that were once good but have now gone off

I'm not talking about a half-finished bottle of Burgundy here, but things like Pret A Manger. Café Rouge. Bill's (the bistro, not the bits of paper). *The Times*. Hampstead. Pimm's. Gucci shoes. France. The list of things that deteriorate tiresomely is endless, and I've no doubt you'll have no difficulty compiling your own if you're at enough of a loose end to wish to do so. Meantime, ask yourself – why haven't things like McDonald's 'gorn off' in the four or five decades since they first invaded our shores? It can't just be that, starting from such a low base, there's nowhere lower left for them to go: after all, Wimpy managed it.

Thongs

Now I'm not talking here about the absurd word Australians substitute for the perfectly adequate 'flip-flops'. No, this is about those peculiar undergarments mostly consisting of a length of string which works its way into the wearer's arse-cheeks. Or btm, for the faint-hearted.

I well remember as a history student reading about the beneficial effect on women's health in the eighteenth century of the near-universalisation of knickers (actually, for a couple of weeks as I recall, I read about little else), so taking the long view, can the spread – apologies for the irony – of thongs be seen as anything other than a step backwards? I mean – look at them! They're all very well on a perfectly proportioned female rear end in a static pose – but on someone other than perfectly proportioned…or in motion…or both?! I rest my case. Well, I would if it weren't for their increasing appearance on males: I don't know about you, but I really DON'T want the hairy-arsed stranger on the adjacent sunbed to be reliant on a flimsy length of gaily-coloured floss to shield me from the horrors that lurk beneath.

See also: Leggings

Three-pin plugs

See The British three-pin plug

Toasters

See Ineffective toasters

Totally over-the-top allergens listings

See Allergies

Tradesmen who diss the efforts of their predecessors

You recognise the syndrome: you've just called a plumber who's arrived at prodigious expense to make a small repair to something ever-so-slightly wrong with your waterworks (no, no, not those – do keep up), and instead of relishing the prospects of an easy little highly rewarded task that will bring him a measure of fulfilment and you a little glow of pleasure, you get the sucking in of breath, whistling between the teeth and the sorry shaking of a head. Tsk tsk tsk, he will go, who on earth did you get to install/mend the last time round/bodge/f★★k up this? Must've been MENTAL. Blah blah blah. What will now almost certainly ensue will be an explanation of how the entire installation will need to be rejigged at – yep – prodigious expense…how it will take a MINIMUM of a week to accomplish…and how the hell are people like the bloody amateur who did the original work allowed to walk the earth unpunished.

And it's not just plumbers. It's the same with motor mechanics and gardeners (whoever pruned that hedge last didn't know the first thing about horticulture, obviously), and in my experience just about every sector of activity known to man. I well recall a series of discussions at, say, three-yearly intervals with a whole series of highly regarded distributors of TV programmes (they're far too cool to be termed salespeople, which is what they actually are, even if the vast majority are largely crap). They always took the same shape: I can't believe that Company X has been so useless at promoting your series around the world… HOW long have they been working for you…?! Well, it's all a bit pathetic isn't it…look we'll first of all go for the low-hanging fruit…there are MASSES of great opportunities out there…it's astonishing that these haven't been grasped…and then we'll really go for it. Blah blah bloody blah. Two or three years later you restart the whole damn process again, already primed to expect an almost identical set of phrases to be wheeled out across the lunch table on the Croisette (at YOUR expense, natch).

And just as with plumbers, motor mechanics and gardeners, you consign your well-deserved world-weariness to the back of your mind and embrace the new relationship and that whiff of optimism that accompanies it. At least with most tradespeople the inevitable eventual disappointment doesn't come with the price of a few magnums of Château Minuty and an exorbitantly overpriced Caesar salad attached – just the outlandish bill and another layer of cynicism to add to the carapace with which you're already equipped.

Trousers

See The wrong (kind of) trousers, Trousers you've just pressed when you realise you've created a 'double-crease'.

Trousers you've just pressed when you realise you've created a 'double-crease'

And once it's done, that's it for good. A pair of perfectly decent trousers ruined by your own incompetence. The motto is simple: one crease good on a trouser-leg, two creases bad. Very bad. And after all that care you thought you had taken with the iron. You'd better resign yourself to the rest of a lifetime wearing chinos, where such niceties don't matter.

Truculent cabbies

What IS it with taxi-drivers that so many think they have a God-given right to give one a hard time the moment you sit back in their cab? Look – it's not my fault that à la Les Dawson you have a problem with your mother-in-law. You'd have thought that in this era of competition from the likes of Uber, they'd be more concerned about what is grandly termed 'customer relations' (hey, even New York yellow cabs have been working on something of a charm offensive in the past decade or so).

Typical was the guy who was SUPPOSED to be driving us all the way from Covent Garden to the Ritz in the pouring rain the day of our ruby wedding anniversary, dressed in our finery. He'd self-evidently given a great deal of thought to the route which would take the longest…involve the worst traffic…and rack up the biggest fare. After half an hour of this I had the temerity to ask if we mightn't go a quicker way, and the mouthful that followed defied belief. 'You obviously don't know that my little boy is dying in hospital of cancer, and I've been on the phone to them for the past half an hour. Some sympathy wouldn't go amiss!' was the gist of it. He hadn't realised that the mike had been left on and we'd heard every goddam syllable. As we got out into the rain to walk the last quarter of a mile, we declined to pay anything, as my wife said, 'I hope you manage to get your Sky contract fixed: that was obviously a very difficult call to them...'

Why can't they all be like the Welshman who picked me up some time ago, so to speak? 'I've just had a meeting with a Welsh guy,' I said, 'and you must be the first Welsh cabbie I've ever met in something like forty years!'

'There are a few of us,' he said, 'not many.'

'Well, here's a funny thing,' I replied. 'The bloke I've just met is called David. David Hard. And all his friends call him Dai. Dai Hard!' Ho ho.

'That is QUITE funny,' he responded, 'but get this, I'm Dai Hard too.' I may not have wet myself at that moment, but it was a close-run thing.

Almost as funny was the time I got a cab driven by a charming Sikh fellow from Leeds Station to a meeting. After a few minutes on the subject of cricket (there was a Test being played at Headingly), in a broad Yorkshire accent overlaid with a hint of the subcontinent, he asked, 'Where are you coming from?' 'London', I replied. 'No, but which country?' he wanted to know. Clearly not 'God's own' given my accent, but I would have thought sixty-plus years of Home Counties living (preceded by being born to into at least the tenth generation of Brits) qualified me as English. Clearly not, but he found the whole thing hilarious.

Truth

TV remote controls

I often hanker after the era pre-1964 when there were only two TV channels in the UK — and not just because all of the hundreds which have invaded us since are near-universally unwatchable. It's the remote control that bothers me, or what in our house is known as 'the black box', even though it's grey and one of a clutch loitering menacingly on top of a cabinet in the living room. Has ANYONE other than a NASA astronaut-in-training ever mastered all the buttons? There are more things to fiddle with than on the steering wheel of a Formula One car, only about three of which I've ever mastered. That's why the print on those buttons has long since disappeared from overuse, reminding me of when, in times past, hitting the key for the letter E on manual typewriters eventually produced nothing more than a smudge.

U

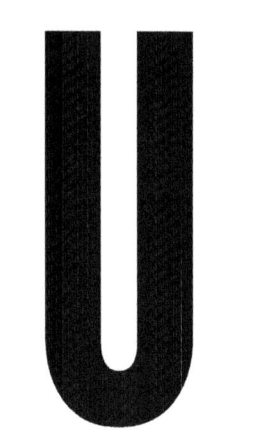

Unpunctuality

See Perennial unpunctuality

Unruly medicine cabinets

What IS it about medicine cabinets that the contents invariably refuse to stay put, but instead take every opportunity to tumble out, when all you've done is to have the temerity to open the door? It's one of life's ironies that things that are MEANT to fall out (like those coins on the sliding thingummy at funfairs that teeter on the edge for a decade without obeying the force of gravity) never do, while things that aren't, fall out at the slightest opportunity.

Unwanted brownfield sites seemingly ripe for development

Have you, like me, peered from your railway carriage from time to time at acres and acres of buddleia- and rubbish-strewn yet otherwise perfectly serviceable (and yes – literally) but redundant land and thought to yourself, 'Why, in this era of desperate shortage of building space, isn't it being used?!' Surely no one is ever going to miss that little derelict rail-side hut or that pile of old sleepers?

And the same goes for all those thousands of acres of drab land lying fallow around countless farms, home to unharvested crops of rusting tractors, ancient trailers, combine harvesters and heaps of rubber tyres (what, by the way, is THAT all about?!).

I suspect that an area the size of Wales could be liberated at in effect zero cost and put to good use.

Updating

There can be few things more infuriating than that baleful little message that crops up on one's computer or mobile phone: updating. You just know that when you click on 'Update and Shut Down' on your PC (accompanied by stern warnings that on no account should you turn it off), that you're in for a long wait while that little clock whirrs for what seems like an eternity, so ensuring that you have no chance whatsoever of making the 18.36 home that you were on a promise to be on. Worse, when your mobile gets it into its head that an update would be fun, you know with a sense of dread that when you come back to use it, all the settings which you've so painstakingly applied will have been reformatted, and half of what you previously did with the click of a finger will now take forever to accomplish – if, that is, it ever works properly again.

Useless corkscrews

When the only function of a corkscrew is to facilitate the easy removal of a cork and thereby permit quick and pain-free access to the contents to which its presence acts as a barrier, you would think that after centuries of cork usage it would not be too taxing to come up with a design that is both foolproof and aesthetically pleasing. How is it, then, that the majority of corkscrews in existence seem to have been developed by adherents to the temperance movement?

Let us first of all dismiss 'waiters' knives'. Has a more fiendish and vile contraption ever been foisted on the drinking classes? I mean, basically, they don't work – especially when the maître d' insists that his staff open the bottle with one WITHOUT RESTING IT ON THE TABLE. This task is as near-impossible to complete as bagging all the Munros in the course of a long weekend. Am I the only restaurant diner to have taken pity on a tearful waitress in mid-failed-opening and offered to take on the assignment for her?

Then there are all those weird and wonderful devices that look more like medieval instruments of torture than instruments designed to bring on pleasure. Forget them.

As well as a foil cutter, what you need is a simple old-fashioned corkscrew with a good-sized wooden handle that firmly grips an 'open' worm – in other words a spiral with a good spike at the end, not something that looks like a miniature hole borer. We once had a 'hole-borer-style' device in the shape of a cherub, which was amusing because the spiral was where another appendage should have been. Sadly, the entertainment value was not matched by its efficacy – that is to say, it didn't fulfil its primary function of extracting a cork. I'd have been better off doing what I've so often had to do in the course of a picnic in the absence of a corkscrew: get hold of a goodish-length strong twig and ram it into the cork, and so the cork into the bottle. Job done.

Utterly absurdly ridiculously unnecessarily long passwords

Can anyone explain why so many bits of electronic kit can only be started up with the use of a password with an ultra-loooong

We all hate passwords dear...but...

sequence mixing letters (upper and lower case, obvs), numbers and special characters that might have defeated the best brains of Bletchley Park? It's only a domestic Wi-Fi for Chrissake – not the key to the United States nuclear arsenal.

V

Vending machines that refuse to deliver the goods

Some vending machines seem to get it into their heads that, rather than merely being passive dispensers of consumer items in return for a small consideration, they are more akin to those machines you sometimes encounter in amusement arcades whereby you insert money and then try to manipulate a small grab crane to 'win' some godawful bit of tat that your offspring have set their heart on. Hence – vending machines with 'attitude', which it seems can themselves decide whether or not to reward your payment and carefully entered code with the delivery of whatever you have alighted on. And of course, they also self-evidently enjoy toying with you, by sometimes not going to the extreme of totally ignoring your request, but simply dispensing an alternative of their own choosing that bears no relation to the choice you yourself made. You can almost hear the damn contraption sniggering, until it realises it's about to get the seventy-third kicking of the day.

It is, of course, possible to enter into the spirit of the proceedings, as was the case with a hot drinks vending machine in the canteen of a long-term client (ironically enough in the flavourings industry). Oh – the fun we had, trying to work out which of the essences had been permed by the supposedly unintelligent machine to produce a new concoction – and what enjoyment was to be had from placing small bets on the outcome. Oxtail soup with a hint of lemon was one particularly pleasing response to the request for a black coffee with sugar, as I recall.

W

Waiting staff with loud, hyper-energetic movements

This behaviour is on a par with those air hostesses who demonstrate their importance by stamping up and down the aisle as loudly as they can in cheap stilettos, so much so that you fear the aircraft structure won't survive intact. You're sitting quietly at lunch, whilst the waiting staff are partly engaged in the demanding assignment of clearing other tables. Rather than employing a few deft, barely noticeable movements to accomplish this, there is a type who insists not just on the heinous tactic of 'stacking at table', but doing so with a flurry of activity and at decibel levels more appropriate to a Greek taverna at the height of the plate-smashing season. And then they stamp backwards and forwards to the kitchen, sounding for all the world like the entire cast of *Riverdance* at a climactic moment. Almost inevitably they will drop several items and collide with another staff member en route, accompanying all this with much heavy sighing, clucking of the tongue and tortured facial expressions, as if to say, 'Look at me...how BUSY and OVERWORKED am I?!?! Wouldn't you be glad to have someone as diligent as me working for you?' Nooooooooooooo!!! Go away and learn from Jeeves how to shimmer, semi-invisibly and definitely inaudibly. Less is, almost invariably, more.

Inadvertently, I obtained empirical proof that this syndrome applies to a 'type'. I once had occasion to visit the lounge at Barcelona airport, where the relative tranquillity was continuously disturbed by the semi-violent actions of the lady who was tasked with taking used crockery etc to the kitchen. Truly, the drama had to be experienced to be believed – and perforce I was there for some hours. Then, believe it or not, some months later I had occasion to revisit the lounge. And there she was, still at it in exactly the same fashion, going at it hammer and tongs. Just extraordinary.

Waste

Look, I'm no eco-warrior, but I have always deplored waste in all its guises. Why is so much food thrown away – by shops and restaurants as well as households? Can't they make a nourishing soup? Why are unoccupied skyscrapers lit up all through the night? Why are shop doors open in winter with all the heat going to warm up the high street – and why are they open in summer with all the aircon going to cool down the high street? Why do people leave their car engines running when they are stationary? Why do people buy half a dozen £10 outfits when two £50 ones would better in every way? Why does every replacement mobile phone need an ever-so-slightly different charger? And why, for God's sake, does everything that's purchased online come packaged in such a multiplicity of heavy-duty cardboard layers, for all the world as if they're wrapped ready for a particularly intense game of pass the parcel?

See also Grotesque over-packaging of things purchased online

Water

See Super-hydration

Weeds

How is it that that expensively bought, lovingly nurtured shrub you chose so carefully from the garden centre spends the rest of its short life glowering at you from its thoroughly fertilised, well-watered spot before withering away to a shrivelled stump, whereas some godforsaken weed can grow to ten feet in a matter of weeks? Bindweed, Japanese knotweed, elder, nettles, buddleia, dockweed,

Don't forget you're going to start weeding the garden... It's taking over

ivy with trunks the thickness of a man's arm – and that vile couch grass that shreds the palm of your hand like a scalpel wielded by a sadistic surgeon: what are they FOR? And why are they in MY garden? You can just about begin to understand why front gardens become carparks and back gardens are done over with decking.

WFH

Was already happening before Covid struck, but then only in the derogatory sense, as in Where the f*** is Wayne? Not working from home again, surely?!', accompanied by a knowing nudge

nudge wink wink. Now a widely accepted practice which its proponents claim is boosting productivity and improving the work-life balance whilst its detractors believe is making the bulk of white-collar workers ever more feckless. For what it's worth, this writer, who has for many years partly 'wfhed', thinks too much of it is all a bit sad, in the eighties sense. But hey ho, WTF.

White wine spritzers

See Badly made spritzers

Wild madder

See Paper cuts

Wine

See Alcohol content of wine, Badly made spritzers, Wine spillages

Wine spillages

Six sheets to the wind – or however many you might be (there are several versions in circulation) – the occasional accidental wine spillage is to be half expected and fully forgiven. But I'm talking here about the unforgivable kind… When a waiter – even a WINE waiter – pours wine into a glass and manages in the process to spill much of the bottle's contents onto the table. Needless to say – well, almost, because I am of course saying it – the wine is invariably red (and as like as not with a high proportion of Syrah and Grenache, thereby making it just about black) and the tablecloth white.

Why CAN'T people like that learn the simple trick that stops this happening? All it takes when the pouring is done is a gentle twist of the bottle neck, held slightly upwards, and the tiniest flick, and ne'er a drop will escape.

And now I'm warming to the theme, how is it possible for a wine waiter to pour a glass of champagne without realising that it is an entirely bubble-free zone and have to be told that it is flat in a way that nature never intended? Even when one has taken the precaution of enquiring beforehand… 'Will it be from a newly-opened bottle?'

See also Incompetent wine pouring

Wires

See Self-tangling wires

Workplaces

See Grim places of work

World-class

What IS all that about? It is surely axiomatic that as soon as anything is described as world-class you KNOW that it is a defence mechanism on the part of the describer (as in that fatuous phrase, 'our Rolls-Royce Civil Service') and that what is being referred to is sure to be second-rate and in fast decline.

X

X-ray airport staff

Humourless, petty officialdom at its horrific worst. If you fly frequently, the oft-repeated instruction to 'check for any liquids, creams or gels' and 'remove iPads from their cases' is nauseating. But even if you don't, the gradual forced removal of half your clothing is demeaning in the extreme: a process made all the worse by the sense that the staff are enjoying it. Whatever evil they had in mind, that bloody shoe-bomber and those wretches from High Wycombe with their exploding Evian bottles had no idea of the grief they would end up inflicting on the world's travellers.

Y

Yawning

See Absurdly dramatic yawning in public

Yobbishness

See Omnipresent yobbishness

Yoghurt

Has anyone ever developed a technique of peeling back the lid of a yoghurt pot in such a way that it doesn't spurt all over your freshly laundered shirt?

Z

Zeitgeist

Making a second appearance in *The Becket List* to illustrate one of the banes of the writer's life: TYPOS. Now THERE'S a First World problem for you. The entry in Vol. I should have read as follows: 'Word currently much overused, especially by those who haven't the foggiest what it means but want to convey the impression that they are in tune with the spirit of the age and have more gravitas than the man on the Clapham omnibus.'

The mangled version that appeared in print more than a little detracted from the sense I was trying to convey, and in fact conveyed no sense whatsoever (so you could argue, was in keeping both with the spirit of the age and the contents of the previous couple of hundred or so pages). Not quite as bad, to be fair, when as a junior account executive in adland I passed for reproduction, in an absurdly high-circulation newspaper (at enormous cost), the ad for the opening of a new furnishing 'superstore' (Europe's largest, WOW) which contained everything but the address, map and phone number, and indeed any hint as to where it might be found. The Client was understandably unamused and I never quite recovered the aforementioned gravitas in that phase of my career, being continuously reminded of my abject failure every time I presented an ad for approval. In fact, I'm not sure I EVER regained any gravitas, since on moving to a new job my new Client insisted on cackling 'HOORAY!' every time I rang and said, 'It's Henry here'. You had to be there…

Acknowledgements

It is self-evidently the case that a second volume of *The Becket List* would not have appeared had it not been for the seeming popularity of the first. So my thanks to all those who bought, read and/or spread the word about the sheer brilliance of Volume I. And also my heartfelt thanks to my excellent publishers, RedDoor Press and in particular Clare Christian and Heather Boisseau, and to my long-suffering editor, Nicky Gyopari.

Some readers – like Frank Martin, Tom Cull, Heather Boisseau, Katie Harrington, Howard Yates, Clodagh Hayes, Sally Burton, Adrian Buttle, Penny Swallow, Paul Jee, Philip Edwards, Jonathan Shapiro, Paul Hornby – have contributed suggestions which I've been very glad to include.

More – such as Instagram's #firstworldproblems postings – have been unashamedly nicked and embellished by me, treading that fine line between inspiration and plagiarism beloved by generations of students.

Many others – friends, erstwhile friends, passing acquaintances, fellow travellers, hostelries, call centres etc etc – have, of course, continued to unwittingly provide inspiration through their unerring ability to irritate. You obviously don't know who you are, but you might of course pick up a clue or two on the way through.